I thank God for making this book possible, I thank my daughters Cherise and Ciarre for always showing me unconditional love, thank you Chris Silva for believing in me and always encouraging me with respect on this journey. Thank you each for inspiring me and choosing me to walk beside you on your journey to success.

~Lisa Christiansen

Your Journey To Self Discovery

There's an old adage that says the journey of a thousand miles begins with a single footstep. Today, I'd like you to take that initial step with me on the journey of your personal empowerment. Start by grabbing a mirror. Now, I would like everyone to hold up the mirror and on a piece of paper write down what you see? Who is that person in the reflection?

The image in the mirror is only a reflection of you but even so it is one of the most powerful images one can see. Who are you? Looking at this mirror and really observing the image is the most important thing you will take away from what I am sharing with you now as we begin your journey to personal empowerment.

I have prayed for only one person and each of you are that one person. Despite all the messages we get bombarded with on television, in fashion magazines and even from that annoying little inner voice, the person you are looking at in the mirror is special. You are enough. Not only are you one of a kind, but also by going on this journey with me you will see that by being the best version of you is truly powerful. You are beautiful. You are strong.

As you accept your authentic self and allow your inner beauty to be reflected I thank you for being that one person God intends for you to be. As you read this please understand that we are now a team of one. Now you can understand we have disproved Einstein's theory that the number one is the loneliest number. One in this sense is anything but lonely. From this day forward always remember if you find yourself by yourself, which is going to happen to all of us, you are not alone. You are not alone because all that you need is within you. Think about the reflection of the person you observed in the mirror. Think about the strengths and special characteristics you wrote down as you looked at the reflection in the mirror.

Now and forever have faith in yourself when ii comes to making a decision. Listen to that inner voice and trust yourself. Are you the person driving a car in the rain that waits until they see two or three other cars with their windshield wipers on to know that it is okay to turn theirs on? If so now is the time for a change, be confident in the individual you are and be the leader.

I would like you to take a piece of paper and write who the most important relationship you've ever had in your life with is? Take a moment and reflect on this question. This doesn't mean that there is a right or wrong answer in the traditional sense. The "right" answer is your answer. By that

I mean what's important to you. Just think about the person that is or was the one that you have the most significant relationship with today and right it down. Everyone who wrote down "me" give yourself a round of applause, If your wrote anything else beginning now commit to take a moment out of your day to make yourself a priority because you are the only one who can decide what you are worth it is only then that others will appreciate your value.

Although there really isn't a wrong answer, the healthiest answer is "you". The most important relationship we will ever have is the one we have with ourselves. Until we can be honest with ourselves, accepting our imperfections which make us perfect, appreciating our dreams, embracing our fears and all the battle scars we've acquired along our life's journey, how can anyone else accept us? How can anyone value you if you don't value yourself? We teach others how to treat us, remember we can't give what we don't have. As unique as we all are one thing we share in common is we often find ourselves emotionally drained from giving and nurturing others in the many roles we find ourselves in which is a beautiful gift. That amazing child within you reflected in the mirror is special and deserves to be nurtured too. By allowing yourself to be important in your life you allow yourself to be a better spouse, a better parent, a better child, and a better friend. You have the emotional constitution to stay in the moment. When you give yourself permission to dream the impossible incredible things happens.

Always remember that information linked to emotion is retained. In life eighty percent is psychology and the other twenty percent are the mechanics. A person who knows where she is going will figure out ways to overcome the challenges along the way. As you walk along your journey of personal empowerment you will have moments, days and perhaps even periods of life in which you will be confronted with frustration. When you are feeling frustrated and overwhelmed, get excited! Frustration only means you are about to have a breakthrough. Likewise confusion also means you are about to learn something, stay excited.

By learning something as you grow from the frustration and confusion you encounter remember that you are developing character and internal wealth. Internal wealth is another way to perceive wisdom. The internal wealth and wisdom that you acquire as you walk down your life's path is what you can give and share with others who come behind you. It is always helpful sharing a concern or struggle with another individual who has experienced it and found a way to break through it. This wealth starts in the mind and in the heart.

Regardless of what your outcome is, pick someone to emulate. Look at the individuals who have found ways to succeed in the areas you are interested in now. Find someone who has a similar passion. Be brave, step up and ask for guidance. Seek a mentor and invest in that relationship. After all, we are the five people we surround ourselves with. Think about that for a moment and decide if those five people are helping you grow or keeping you stuck. Once you answer that question, take action.

Define where you are. Determine what can be done in a day, a week and a month to move you further a long your journey to reach the outcome you identified for yourself. Write your outcome in detail. Write your outcome in lots of places so that you will focus on it. Our daily focus either moves us toward or away from our outcome so be proactive. Because the most important relationship you have with another person is the relationship you have with that amazing person in the mirror, make it a priority to focus on your outcome daily. One way in which you can accomplish this is to set your outcome is if it is already happened. There's a nugget of truth in that old saying fake it until you make it. "Act as if until" you have already achieved your outcome or as if you are currently living it.

Keep your focus. Success is the only option that is acceptable. Set another outcome as soon as your goal is met. Always take your outcome and make it manageable by dividing it into bite size pieces.

Love like you've never been hurt. Keep in mind that the angrier you get the more static in your brain. The more static in your brain the less you can hear what's being said to you. Thus, so remember to live and love as love truly conquers all. May the love you have hidden deep within your heart find its way to the love in your dreams. Make the laughter that you find in your tomorrow wipe away the pain you find in your yesterdays.

Staying in love is a decision. Loving and valuing yourself is also a decision and it's not always easy. Anger, tears and laughter are all expected and okay in an interpersonal relationship. Through it all trust that you are truly in love. When you love yourself you have an abundance of love. Remember, love is a gift that you give without expectation of its return. It is then that your true love shines through and that is when you really know that what is inside of you, your inner wealth, your inner wisdom, and inner love is all that you need. The good news is that all of those gifts are already within you.

By learning to love myself and recognize the gifts that are within me, I am confident and secure enough to encourage you to step out in faith by looking at the person you are today, seeing where you are and deciding where you want to be. Because I am walking my own journey of self discovery I can tell you that yes, you'll get frustrated and confused and those are all good things. I can't say I always knew the woman I saw in the mirror what I can say is I have always appreciated this woman and her unique abilities because of the mentors that I have been blessed to have walk in front of me and beside me, I am the woman that I am today because of you. For those of you who know me from thank God I volume 3 I would like to take this opportunity to thank you with my deepest gratitude for allowing me to share my challenges that I encountered on my journey to personal empowerment. Thank you for accepting me for who I am. I have a long road ahead of me and that's exciting. Now as I walk victoriously, I encourage you to walk beside me through my own personal awakening. Today I come to you with the opportunity to share with you my appreciation and love for you.

What has my journey taught me so far? From the seeds of necessity grows success. From the sweat of desperation come the seeds of purpose. Let's have some fun as we grow together walking along our path recognizing that we're never really alone, that we have all of the skills we need to get us through today within us. Trust that whatever tomorrow brings will be okay because you have the skills and tools from your own inner wealth, wisdom and love to make it.

Everyone has a primary question, what is yours? Mine is "what ACTion will I take today to create the tomorrow I am committed to living". Equally as important, how can you create a destination that will allow you to be authentic to the complex, talented and ever growing gift that you are? Live in strength by making the situations you experience on your journey of personal empowerment into opportunities to serve others and yourself.

4 Keys to a Successful Partnership with the One You Love

A Lasting, Fulfilling Relationship – The "Dynamic of Stay": 4 Keys to a Successful Partnership with the One You Love

It is currently my honest belief that more people in the world are mystified regarding how to find - and keep love - than how to find and keep money. There was a time in my life I believed the opposite to be true. There was a day when I believed that "money" and "wealth" was the prevalent concern in the minds of most. I now believe I was wrong.

Every day, the majority of questions I get - and hear - revolve around what constitutes "true love" and what creates the "Dynamic of Stay" in a relationship. The "Dynamic of Stay" I am referring to here is the study of what makes some couples stay together, no matter what obstacles and issues they might face, versus others who go their separate ways when faced with even minor crisis.

Before I begin to delve into the answer to this question, first, let us clarify that in order for the "Dynamic of Stay" to even be applicable, we have to be discussing a "good" relationship. In other words, a relationship that is fundamentally sound and where there are not major issues such as:

Abuse (mental or physical) directed to the partner and/or children

Substance dependency that is not actively being addressed by the dependent individual

Repeated, blatant, and unrepentant infidelity

Now, I am not saying any of the above scenarios is always and absolutely “hopeless” either. What I am saying, is that if any of the above apply to your relationship, I strongly encourage you to find a professional you can trust with whom to discuss your particular situation because there are things that need to be addressed and “fixed” before the 4 Keys I am going to discuss below will be applicable for you.

Okay, with that out of the way, what creates the “Dynamic of Stay” in our love relationships? It’s really very simple. Throughout time, the greatest teachers have told us the answers many times over. Maybe we didn’t pay attention. Maybe we just didn’t want to hear the answers or we weren’t ready. Regardless, we have always had these keys at our disposal. We just needed to open our eyes, open our ears, and open - and prepare - our heart to receive the answers and then do what we needed to do to make them work in our lives.

The crux – or main point – to achieving this dynamic with your partner is understanding who – and what – takes priority in your lives and in what order. Additionally, both partners must be committed to understanding and fulfilling the necessary strategies to create the "Dynamic of Stay" as well. Thus, the ideal time to discuss these keys is before making the decision to partner forever with someone. However, it is never too late. Even in a struggling partnership or marriage, if both partners are really vested in making it work, discussing these keys – and agreeing to practice them and enact them in your lives from this point forward – could just be the glue you need to make it through whatever storm you are facing.

The simple fact is: Those who get the "Dynamic of Stay" right very seldom "give up" on their partner or relationship and go on to live long, fulfilling, lives together. Those who get it wrong very often end up leaving and go on to repeat the cycle of finding love and then losing it over and over.

Key #1 – God First

I know some of you reading this might not agree with me and that's okay. I realize there are exceptions to this principle but they are just that - "exceptions" - and this has been proven over and over. Just like "winning the lottery" is sometimes the exception to the "equal value; equal exchange" principle. How many people really want to leave their relationships in the hands of "lottery-type" odds? Yeah, not me either.

Studies have shown that the majority of couples who "last" despite what life throws at them - those who "stay" - routinely credit God for being the focal point in their relationship. This doesn't necessarily mean they are in church every time the doors are open. This doesn't even mean that their God is the same as your God or my God. What it does mean is that they have a Supreme Being they feel accountable to and that accountability holds them in check throughout most - and in every area - of their lives. As such, their belief in "God" dictates how they think and behave, not only personally but also in their relationship with others. They also often feel that God has been faithful in his commitment to them and it is their responsibility to be faithful to their commitment to their partner in return. You know the saying "What Would Jesus Do? (WWJD)" I believe this became so popular because people with a strong faith do often ask themselves when faced with a tough decision, “What Would Jesus Do?” or “What Would God Do?” Thus, this usually results in a greater compassion and understanding for their partner. Instead of seeking to stay in anger and blame, they seek to forgive. Instead of seeking an “out”, they seek something - anything - to make them stay “in”.

Key #2 - Your “We” Second

We are taught from the time we are little, often inadvertently and subconsciously, to look out for #1 - ourselves. Over and over we hear expressions like, “If you don’t look out for yourself, no one else will.” Or “No one else is responsible for your happiness but you.”

Right now even, many of you are likely thinking, “Yes...what is wrong with that? It’s the truth, right?”

The answer is “Yes,” but also, “No.”

When we are growing up and learning and

absorbing and becoming our "adult self", these statements do have merit. When it is "just us", we need to learn to put ourselves first. We need to learn to accept responsibility for our mental well-being, happiness, and success so that we can become independent, self-driven, productive, human beings.

However, when we partner "for life", a shift is supposed to happen. When you agree to share your life with someone through your marriage vows, you are theoretically becoming "one". This is what the Bible teaches. This is what Universal Law teaches. If you are one, decisions should be made and actions should be taken, from that position as "one". There is no more, "What is best for me?" but rather, "What is best for us?" There is no more "I have to make myself happy," but rather, "What will make us happy?"

If you are tempted to doubt this right now, I will step out on a limb and say that until you believe this to be true, your chances for a lifelong union are going to be slim. If your relationship lasts forever - if it demonstrates the "Dynamic of Stay", you will be the exception.

Think about it this way…

Did you ever play with colored clay or play dough when you were a kid? Imagine you are red and your partner is purple. Separate, you are these bright, brilliant, colors. Now, imagine you are blended together. When this happens to colored clay, you can no longer call what is created "purple" or "red". It is something totally new. Can you ever split this clay back up to be "red" or "purple" alone? No, it will always be this new "color" or "blend of colors".

Now, of course, the colored clay had no "choice" in the matter. But if both parties in a relationship imagine their union as this permanent blending of colors – before the union ever takes place – you might go into that union with a more permanent mindset. Then, if you make decisions in your relationship, in your life together, with the understanding that you can't ever be split apart – or that if you are, you are going to be messy and very much unlike your original self – it will affect every single one of those decisions. Just this one simple mindset change on behalf of both parties – hopefully before, but even after – a lifelong love partnership is ever entered into, will totally change the place from which choices are made throughout that relationship. And if choices are made with the idea of "Will this keep us - or even bring us closer - together?" instead of "Will this tear us apart?", the "Dynamic of Stay" is much more inevitable.

Key #3 - Your Children Third

Whether they are yours, his/hers, or someone else's altogether - children in a "good" relationship (see above for definition) should always come behind God and behind the "we". Unless we are discussing a situation where children are in mental or physical danger, their happiness and well-being should not ever be considered above that of your spouse/partner. Before this upsets some of you, let me explain...

The reason for this is short and sweet. When partners allow themselves to be torn apart or divided by the wants, whims, and desires of their children, they have lost sight of Key #2 - Focus on the "We". This is not to say that loving and devoted couples will never disagree on the best decisions to make or actions to take regarding their children. It is to say you don't do that in front of the children. And you don't ever let it divide you to the point where you have lost sight of the importance of the "we" of the two of you. Thus, you make decisions about your children in private and then when those decisions are agreed upon, you present them as a united front and support one another in those decisions fully. Furthermore, you don't allow yourselves to get played against the other or to be persuaded to take an opposite stand or action than that which you agreed upon together.

Interestingly, little children (and even teens and young adults) see their parents or guardians with whom they live and/or are being raised as "one" anyway. When they are able to tear that apart (and they will try because they are kids - not fully mature yet - and as such, want to try to "get their way), it usually makes them more unhappy than happy. Often, they don't even know why. They just know that something doesn't feel right. Believe it or not, there is little that is more beneficial to the well-being and long-term success of a child than having parents who stand together as one single unit that will not be turned upon itself or split apart. This is also the greatest thing you can do to ensure the future success of their relationships because there is no greater teacher of Key #2 and Key #3 than seeing it in action over and over when you are little yourself.

Key #4 – Self Last

This is simple. Once you have entered into a lifelong union and made that commitment to your partner "forever", "for richer or poorer, sickness and in health", you live it. You do it. Even when it doesn't "feel good" or you don't "feel like it". Even when something better seems to come along or tempts you off your path. You think, "What would God do?" or "What is best for the 'we' that is 'us'?" or "How would this affect my children?" You stop thinking about what you want right now or what feels good at this moment and you think about the promises you have made and the priorities you agreed to when you made those promises. And then you do it. And you keep doing it. And pretty soon, the questions and temptations stop coming because you don't let them in. Or maybe they don't stop coming but you stop noticing. That is when the "Dynamic of Stay" has become a part of your life and the bond that will hold your love relationship together forever.

All a woman wants is to know that you are going to be there no matter what. And no matter what means no matter what.

Success Without Fulfillment is Failure

We give words meaning, we define what success is, and we create our own destiny based on our own internal blueprint.

Today, people feel a lot of unnecessary and unneeded stress caused by comparing themselves to others. This stress puts a toll on both their mental and physical health. In fact, even theCDC says that "emotional health" can be up to 85% responsible for physical health.

First, you must understand that your physical surroundings determine who you "hang" with and who you "hang" with is a large determinant of your self-worth. You are a reflection of your five closest friends. This is because we as social creatures tend to base our opinions of ourselves on comparisons between ourselves and those in our immediate circles. This can work both for you and against you. Surrounding yourself with others who have achieved things - and a level of success - you desire to achieve, gives you examples after which to model your behavior. On the other hand, if you are constantly comparing yourselves to these people, that can cause you immense stress.

Thus, this is a highly individualized matter that you must consider on a personal level and how these comparisons affect you in particular.

Some people need to be "reaching up" to be motivated. While others need to excel within their personal group to feel confident enough to eventually reach up. It is a fine balance. That is why we will be examining this subject over the next couple of weeks from both angles but we'll hit on a quick summary now...

If you are one who gets stressed by comparing yourself to your more successful friends, neighbors, or co-workers, one of the quickest ways to change any negative feelings, jealousy, or status envy you might have is to ensure you also have people who are at your current socio-economic and enviro-economic status in your circle as well.

This idea was put forth in "How to Get Over Status Anxiety" atwww.psychologytoday.com. This is not to imply that you necessarily change your circle of friends. It's just that you need to be more conscientious of who you compare yourself to on a regular basis.

For example, you can seek out those you can better and more appropriate identify with through social and civic groups. And sometimes, one can better flourish by seeking out "smaller settings" in which to work and play as well. Sometimes successes are easier to come by and recognize in such a setting. You must also learn to recognize your own successes - in their own right - and use them to balance what you feel are you failures or shortcomings that only exist in comparison to others. Especially comparisons to others who might have more advantages - or resources - than you do at your disposal.

Perhaps most importantly, learn to use this "envy" for good. Use it to propel you to greater heights. Instead of thinking, "Poor me. I don't have..." or "I'll never be able to do what so-and-so did because I didn't grow up rich" or "I'm not as educated so I am not as smart as...", and letting those things get you down on yourself, begin to consider how your particular circumstances served you. Only you havethe power to decide that. Has a lack of certain things in your life forced you to be resourceful? Has your lack of money in your life put you in a position to empathize with those facing certain problems that only you - with your underprivileged or even middle-class background - can really understand? Maybe your lack of formal education has driven you to really study the world - or independently - so that you actually have more practical knowledge than your more "classroom educated" counterparts?

On the other hand, if you are someone who needs

to be consistently challenged to strive for "more", then add people to your circle of influence who are currently where you desire to be and mirror them. This will take years off your journey to success and allow you to arrive at your destination in a much shorter time. There are always two sides to every coin and while some need to remain secure in their current situation - and there is nothing wrong with that if that is what gives you greater emotional security and satisfaction - I, on the other hand, am always searching for growth.

I believe that wherever you are at some point in time, you have made an "appointment" to be there.Being "wealthy" isn't just a question of how much money you have, but rather having what you want. It has been said by many that success without fulfillment is failure. Wealth isn't absolute, it's relative to desire... SELF ESTEEM= success divided by expectation. Meaning, people base their self-worth on their definition of success. To be successful, one must be prepared for opportunity and then answer the door when it knocks - or lower your expectation - either way decide what works for you.

For today, the key here is remembering that everything in life serves you equally. Aside from the other practical steps mentioned above, your attitude - and view - on these things, can change your life as much as (or more!) than anything. For the next few weeks, we will cover this more intricately. In the meantime, remember that success – for you – is merely a matter of how you define it. What is your definition of "success"?

With Love And Gratitude,
~Lisa Christiansen

Mastery

Mastery in one's career and self growth simply requires that we consistently and constantly produce results beyond the ordinary into the extraordinary by producing outstanding results. Mastery is attained by consistently stepping outside of our comfort zone, going beyond our limits with the knowledge that the only limits there are in life are the ones we set for ourselves. Open your eyes, listen to hear, feel your achievement and breakthrough your limits to the success you deserve. For most people, this starts with technical excellence in a chosen field and a commitment to that excellence. This needs to begin with a clear vision and the decision to do what it takes making success your only option. If you are willing to commit yourself to excellence, to surround yourself with things that represent excellence, your life will change because you are your five closest friends. (When we speak of miracles, we speak of events or experiences that go beyond the ordinary into the extraordinary.)

It's remarkable how much mediocrity we live with, surrounding ourselves with daily reminders that the average is the acceptable, we must decide this behavior of mediocrity is UNACCEPTABLE. More often than not you will find

the common belief is limited thinking with a mindset of go to school to get a good job to retire comfortable and then you die. I urge you to look inside yourself and identify the things that are keeping you powerless to go beyond any "limit" that you have arbitrarily set for yourself, take a moment to assess all of these things around you that promote your being "average", now take action to remove these things from your life even if this means making new friends, because often your friends will bring guilt to your dreams by saying "oh, you think you are better than me?" or "what makes you think you can do that?" these are dream thieves and you need dream achievers in your circle of friends, with that being said you must reach up to those that frighten you and cultivate friendships where you once thought were impossible you will be surprised how many will be excited to mentor you. To begin mastery is to remove everything in your environment that represents mediocrity, removing those things that are limiting. Again, one way is to surround yourself with friends who ask more of themselves than anyone else ever would because these are the ones who step up to defy the odds, to set new standards and to be the change they want to see in this world by being the example. It is this recipe for success that you must emulate to achieve your success because if you find someone who is successfully doing what you are passionate about you simply have to follow their formula to achieve the same result.

Another step on the path to mastery is the removal of resentment toward masters whether on your level, below or above your level, this action is very important because these are your potential mentors. We are always learning from each other so respect is critical, if you don't respect the person please respect their gifts to contribute to others even if you don't agree. Develop humility so that while in the presence of masters you are emotionally available with an open heart and an open mind to grow from the experience. Do not compare yourself to others and do not resent people who have mastery, remain open, respectful and receptive; allow the experience to enrich you like the planting of a seed within you that, with nourishment, will grow into your own individual unique mastery.

We are all created equal, mastery is learned through education, life experiences and the examples laid before us. A true master will embrace their flaws and weaknesses as a tool to relate to others with a genuine appreciation of their circumstances. A master recognizes this fault as a foundation for building the extraordinary instead of using it as an excuse for inactivity, use this as a vehicle for growing, which is essential in the process of attaining mastery. You must be able to learn, grow and accept criticism without condemning yourself to accept results and improve upon them. Growth is essential to power and mastery because if you are not growing you are dying.

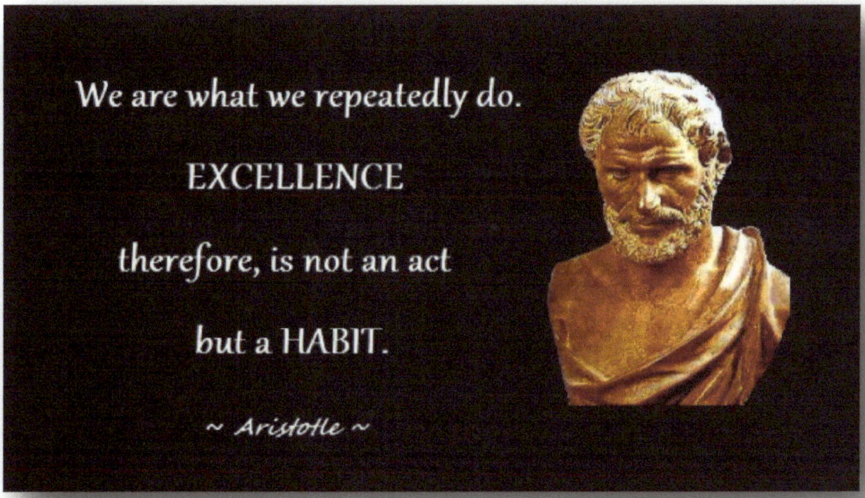

Reality and Intentions

Your reality is created by your intentions

An intention is a quality of consciousness that you bring to an action.

At each moment you choose the intentions that will shape your experiences and those things upon which you will focus your attention. If you choose unconsciously, you will evolve unconsciously. if you choose consciously, you will evolve consciously.

Every action, thought, and feeling is motivated by an intention and that intention is a cause that exists as one with an effect. If we participate in the cause, it is not possible for us not to participate in the effect or as I like to say if I take the blame I will also take the credit. In this most profound way we are held responsible for our every action, thought, and feeling, which is to say, for our every intention. I would like to re-define the meaning of the word responsible; responsibility is the “ability to respond.” Taking responsibility in all situations puts you in control. Many people, when confronted with challenges, sometimes to fall into a victim mindset. It is as though they are trapped and can't do anything to change their environment. Taking responsibility gives you power over yourself and your circumstances.

From the perception of the five sensory human, intentions have no effects, the effects of actions are physical, and not all actions affect others or us. What does affect us are our six human needs and the way we anchor our triggers.

From the perception of the multi sensory human the intention behind an action determines its effects, every intention affects both us and others and the effects of intentions extend far beyond the physical world.

Feel your intentions in your heart, feel not what your mind tells you, but what your heart tells you.

Intuition is perception beyond the physical senses that is meant to assist you. It is that sensory system which operates without data from the five senses and is driven by our six human needs of certainty, uncertainty, significance, love/connection, growth, and contribution.

What is behind our eyes holds more power that what is in front of them, the brain and it's connection to the heart. When in a state of gratitude it is in rhythmic synchronization or better said it is the only time it is in a state of complete harmony.

The decisions that you make and the actions that you take upon the Earth are the means by which you evolve.

An angry personality will respond to the difficulties of life with anger, and thereby bring into being the necessity of experiencing the results of anger.

A person who is angry, and yet reveres life, however, will respond very differently to the difficulties of his or her life than a person who is angry and has no reverence for life.

Each personality draws to itself personalities with consciousness of like frequency, or like weakness, therefore, the world of an angry person is filled with angry people, the world of a greedy person is filled with greedy people, and a loving person lives in a world of loving people. Look at your surroundings because you are your five closest peers.

Until you become aware of the effects of your anger, you will continue to be an angry person.

Knowledge is NOT power, clarity is power and for each level of knowledge you must make the time to become clear in your outcome because you are held responsible for how you use it. Remember, responsible means the ability to respond.

How will you choose to live and whom will you surround yourself with? Reach up to mentors and you will be surprised who will be excited to empower you on your journey to enrich the lives of others which in turn drives you to your outcome as it was best said by Zig Ziglar "when you help others get to where they want to be you will get to where you want to be".

Heart-Brain Synchronization

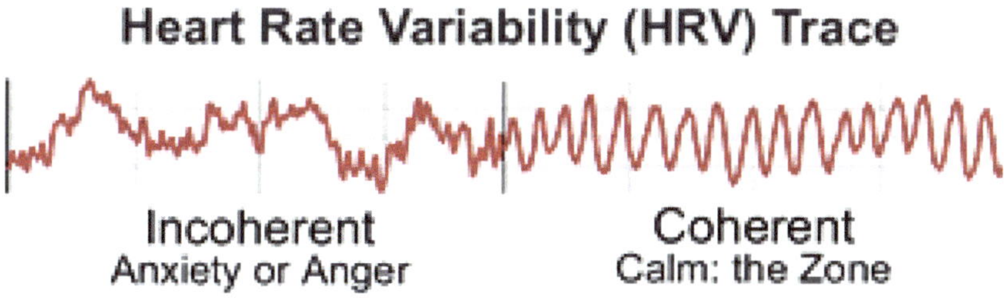

Heart-Brain Synchronization

Lisa Christiansen

The research team at Stanford University has shown that techniques which combine intentional heart focus with the generation of sustained positive feelings lead to a beneficial mode of physiological function they have termed psycho-physiological coherence. Correlates of psycho-physiological coherence include a sine wavelike pattern in the heart rhythms, increased heart-brain synchronization (alpha rhythms become more synchronized to the heart) and entrainment between the heart's rhythmic patterns, respiration, blood pressure rhythms, and other physiological systems. Although psycho-physiological coherence is a natural state that can occur spontaneously while people are feeling genuine positive emotions and during sleep, sustained periods are generally rare.

During states of psycho-physiological coherence, our inner systems function with a higher degree of synchronization, efficiency and harmony, which correlates with improved emotional stability, quality of emotional experience, health, and cognitive performance. HeartMath studies conducted across diverse populations have associated increased psycho-physiological coherence with reduced anxiety and depression, decreased physical symptoms of stress, enhanced immunity, reduced cortisol, and increased DHEA. IHM has collaborated with Stanford University and other institutions in studies, which have shown that heart centered techniques and psycho-physiological coherence facilitate the body's healing processes and improve physical health outcomes. For example, improvements in clinical status have been demonstrated in individuals with hypertension, diabetes, congestive heart failure, asthma and AIDS.

With practice you learn how to shift into coherence at will, even in difficult situations that previously would have drained your emotional vitality and buoyancy. You will readily see and experience changes in your heart rhythm patterns as you practice emotional regulation techniques. Your heart rhythms generally become less irregular, and sine wavelike as you send more heartfelt love and appreciation through your system.

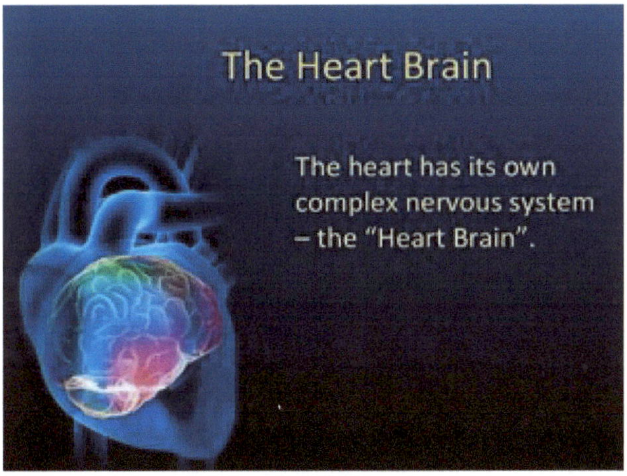

Authentic Empowerment

When we align our thoughts, emotions, and actions with the highest part of ourselves, we are filled with enthusiasm, purpose and meaning. Life is rich and full. We have no thoughts of bitterness, we have no memory of fear. We are joyously and intimately engaged with our world, this is the experience of authentic power because Perception is reality. you give words and actions meaning, change your belief and you will change your future. Once you master your emotions you are in control of your destiny, conquer the mind and your body will follow. It is when you make a change in your psychology that you will create a much-needed change in your physiology. TAKE CONTROL NOW!!!

Your perception creates the reality that you experience, until you become aware of this it happens unconsciously, therefore, be mindful of what you project. You must stand guard at the doorway of your mind because this is the first step toward authentic power.

The journey to authentic power requires that you become conscious of all that you feel and take immediate action, because any action that moves you in the direction of your desired outcome is "on the right track" as progress only happens when a decision is made, just remember the definition of decision is to cut off, to sever, leaving no other option or alternative. Just remember the story of troy, find your driving force, your leverage, and be resolved in your commitment.

When seen through authentically empowered eyes a being with a higher rank in creation is one that has more ability to see without obstruction, more ability to live in love and wisdom, more ability and desire to help others evolve to own their own power.

When you consciously invoke growing you consciously invoke the parts of yourself that are not whole to come into the foreground of your life. With each recurrence of anger, jealousy, or fear, you are given the choice to challenge it or to give into it. Each time you step up to new challenges and grow by setting new standards it loses power and you gain power.

As you choose to empower yourself the temptation that you challenge will surface again and again building a stronger more resilient you. With each choice that you make to align yourself with the energy of your soul you empower yourself. Authentic power is built up step-by-step, choice-by-choice and it must be earned. First we make our choices then our choices make us.

What decision will you make today to create the tomorrow you are committed to?

I will first give thanks to God for blessing me as I awake each day and before I choose to make any decision I will ask myself these 10 questions:

1) What am I doing today to get what I want?
2) Will this behavior improve my situation and move me towards what I want?... or am I settling?
3) How would the person I want to be do the thing I am about to do?
4) Who do I have to become to attract the success

I want?
5) Am I willing to accept the consequences of not changing.
6) Who is in control?
7) Am I practicing to improve or doing just enough to get by?
8) What don't I SEE?
9) If my Board of Directors could see my level of effort, focus and intensity, would I get a raise or get fired?
10) Am I willing to do whatever it takes?

By remaining in your power you do not become a static energy system, one that hoards energy to itself. You become a stable energy system, capable of conscious acts of focus and intention. You become a magnet for those who are illuminated and those who want to be outstanding.

You cannot and will not encounter a circumstance or a single moment that does not serve directly and immediately the need of your soul to heal, to become whole.

When presented the challenging dynamic of the human experience Jesus encountered the Luciferic principle. When he was offered dominion over the entire globe was he tempted? Yes he was tempted! If he were not there would have been no power in his choice. Authentic empowerment

is not gained by making choices that do not stretch you. Sooner or later, each soul will turn toward authentic power. Every situation serves this goal and every soul will reach it. When you understand that the experiences of your life are necessary to the balancing of the energy of your soul you are free to not react to them personally and instead respond with a fine balance of logic and emotion. Although what you encounter and what you do in each moment is appropriate and perfect to the evolution of your soul, the shape of the experiences of your life is determined by the choices that you make. Will you choose to linger in resentment, to remain enveloped in grief for a life half lived or will you decide to release these lower frequency currents of energy in exchange for a life filled with gratitude for the love, acceptance and significance that brings respect and a legacy fruitful of fulfillment.

Emotional Intelligence Central

Emotional Intelligence Central

Dr. Lisa Christine Christiansen

Strategies and Tips for Good Mental Health, I will give you the tools for lasting results.

People who are emotionally healthy are in control of their emotions and their behavior. They are able to handle life's inevitable challenges, build strong relationships, and lead productive, fulfilling lives. When bad things happen, they're able to bounce back and move on.

Unfortunately, too many people take their mental and emotional health for granted – focusing on it only when they develop problems. But just as it requires effort to build or maintain physical health, so it is with mental and emotional health. The more time and energy you invest in your emotional health, the stronger it will be. The good news is that there are many things you can do to boost your mood, build resilience, and get more enjoyment out of life.

What is mental health or emotional health?

Mental or emotional health refers to your overall psychological well-being. It includes the way you feel about yourself, the quality of your relationships, and your ability to manage your feelings and deal with difficulties.

Good mental health isn't just the absence of mental health problems. Being mentally or emotionally healthy is much more than being free of depression, anxiety, or other psychological issues. Rather than the absence of mental illness, mental and emotional health refers to the presence of positive characteristics.

People who are mentally and emotionally healthy have:

- A sense of contentment.

- A zest for living and the ability to laugh and have fun.

- The ability to deal with stress and bounce back from adversity.

- A sense of meaning and purpose, in both their activities and their relationships.

- The flexibility to learn new things and adapt to change.

- A balance between work and play, rest and activity, etc.

- The ability to build and maintain fulfilling relationships.

- Self-confidence and high self-esteem.

These positive characteristics of mental and emotional health allow you to participate in life to the fullest extent possible through productive, meaningful activities and strong relationships. These positive characteristics also help you cope when faced with life's challenges and stresses.

The role of resilience in mental and emotional health

Being emotionally and mentally healthy doesn't mean never going through bad times or experiencing emotional problems. We all go through disappointments, loss, and change. And while these are normal parts of life, they can still cause sadness, anxiety, and stress.

The difference is that people with good emotional health have an ability to bounce back from adversity, trauma, and stress. This ability is called resilience. People who are emotionally and mentally healthy have the tools for coping with difficult situations and maintaining a positive outlook. They remain focused, flexible, and creative in bad times as well as good.

One of the key factors in resilience is the ability to balance your emotions. The capacity to recognize your emotions and express them appropriately helps you avoid getting stuck in depression, anxiety, or other negative mood states. Another key factor is having a strong support network. Having trusted people you can turn to for encouragement and support will boost your resilience in tough times.

Building your resilience

Resilience involves maintaining flexibility and balance in your life as you deal with stressful circumstances and traumatic events. This happens in several ways, including:

- Letting yourself experience strong emotions, and also realizing when you may need to avoid experiencing them at times in order to continue functioning

- Stepping forward and taking action to deal with your problems and meet the demands of daily living, and also stepping back to rest and reenergize yourself

- Spending time with loved ones to gain support and encouragement, and also nurturing yourself

- Relying on others, and also relying on yourself

Source: American Psychological Association

Physical health is connected to mental and emotional health

Taking care of your body is a powerful first step towards mental and emotional health. The mind and the body are linked. When you improve your physical health, you'll automatically experience greater mental and emotional well-being. For example, exercise not only strengthens our heart and lungs, but also releases endorphins, powerful chemicals that energize us and lift our mood.

The activities you engage in and the daily choices you make affect the way you feel physically and emotionally.

- Get enough rest. To have good mental and emotional health, it's important to take care of your body. That includes getting enough sleep. Most people need seven to eight hours of sleep each night in order to function optimally.

- Learn about good nutrition and practice it. The subject of nutrition is complicated and not always easy to put into practice. But the more you learn about what you eat and how it affects your energy and mood, the better you can feel.

- Exercise to relieve stress and lift your mood. Exercise is a powerful antidote to stress, anxiety, and depression. Look for small ways to add activity to your day, like taking the stairs instead of the elevator or going on a short walk. To get the most mental health benefits, aim for 30 minutes or more of exercise per day.

• Get a dose of sunlight every day. Sunlight lifts your mood, so try to get at least 10 to 15 minutes of sun per day. This can be done while exercising, gardening, or socializing.

• Limit alcohol and avoid cigarettes and other drugs.

Improve mental and emotional health by taking care of yourself

In order to maintain and strengthen your mental and emotional health, it's important to pay attention to your own needs and feelings. Don't let stress and negative emotions build up. Try to maintain a balance between your daily responsibilities and the things you enjoy. If you take care of yourself, you'll be better prepared to deal with challenges if and when they arise.

Tips and strategies for taking care of yourself:

• Appeal to your senses. Stay calm and energized by appealing to the five senses: sight, sound, touch, smell, and taste. Listen to music that lifts your mood, place flowers where you will see and smell them, massage your hands and feet, or sip a warm drink.

• Engage in meaningful, creative work. Do things that challenge your creativity and make you feel productive, whether or not you get paid for it -

things like gardening, drawing, writing, playing an instrument, or building something in your workshop.

• Get a pet. Yes, pets are a responsibility, but caring for one makes you feel needed and loved. There is no love quite as unconditional as the love a pet can give. Animals can also get you out of the house for exercise and expose you to new people and places.

• Make leisure time a priority. Do things for no other reason than that it feels good to do them. Go to a funny movie, take a walk on the beach, listen to music, read a good book, or talk to a friend. Doing things just because they are fun is no indulgence. Play is an emotional and mental health necessity.

• Make time for contemplation and appreciation. Think about the things you're grateful for. Mediate, pray, enjoy the sunset, or simply take a moment to pay attention to what is good, positive, and beautiful as you go about your day.

Everyone is different; not all things will be equally beneficial to all people. Some people feel better relaxing and slowing down while others need more activity and more excitement or stimulation to feel better. The important thing is to find activities that you enjoy and that give you a boost.

Limit unhealthy mental habits like worrying

Try to avoid becoming absorbed by repetitive mental habits - negative thoughts about yourself and the world that suck up time, drain your energy, and trigger feelings of anxiety, fear, and depression.

Manage your stress levels

Stress takes a heavy toll on mental and emotional health, so it's important to keep it under control. While not all stressors can be avoided, stress management strategies can help you brings things back into balance.

For tips on how to reduce, prevent, and cope with stress, see

Supportive relationships: The foundation of emotional health

No matter how much time you devote to improving your mental and emotional health, you will still need the company of others to feel and be your best. Humans are social creatures with emotional needs for relationships and positive connections to others.. We're not meant to survive, let alone thrive, in isolation. Our social brains crave companionship—even when experience has made us shy and distrustful of others.

Tips and strategies for connecting to others:

• Get out from behind your TV or computer screen. Screens have their place but they will never have the same effect as an expression of interest or a reassuring touch. Communication is a largely nonverbal experience that requires you to be in direct contact with other people, so don't neglect your real-world relationships in favor of virtual interaction.

• Spend time daily, face-to-face, with people you like. Make spending time with people you enjoy a priority. Choose friends, neighbors, colleagues, and family members who are upbeat, positive, and interested in you. Take time to inquire about people you meet during the day that you like.

• Volunteer. Doing something that helps others has a beneficial effect on how you feel about yourself. The meaning and purpose you find in helping others will enrich and expand your life. There is no limit to the individual and group volunteer opportunities you can explore. Schools, churches, nonprofits, and charitable organization of all sorts depend on volunteers for their survival.

• Be a joiner. Join networking, social action, conservation, and special interest groups that meet on a regular basis. These groups offer wonderful opportunities for finding people with common interests – people you like being with who are potential friends.

Building Great Relationships

If you find it difficult to connect to others or to maintain fulfilling, long-term relationships, you may benefit from raising your emotional intelligence. Emotional intelligence allows us to communicate clearly, "read" other people, and resolve conflicts.

Risk factors for mental and emotional problems

Your mental and emotional health has been and will continue to be shaped by your experiences. Early childhood experiences are especially

significant. Genetic and biological factors can also play a role, but these too can be changed by experience.

Risk factors that can compromise mental and emotional health:

• Poor connection or attachment to your primary caretaker early in life. Feeling lonely, isolated, unsafe, confused, or abused as an infant or young child.

• Traumas or serious losses, especially early in life. Death of a parent or other traumatic experiences such as war or hospitalization.

• Learned helplessness. Negative experiences that lead to a belief that you're helpless and that you have little control over the situations in your life.

• Illness, especially when it's chronic, disabling, or isolates you from others.

• Side effects of medications, especially in older people who may be taking a variety of medications.

• Substance abuse. Alcohol and drug abuse can both cause mental health problems and make preexisting mental or emotional problems worse.

Whatever internal or external factors have shaped your mental and emotional health, it's never too late to make changes that will improve your psychological well-being. Risk factors can be counteracted with protective factors, like strong relationships, a healthy lifestyle, and coping strategies for managing stress and negative emotions.

When to seek professional help for emotional problems

If you've made consistent efforts to improve your mental and emotional health and you still don't feel good - then it's time to seek professional help. Because we are so socially attuned, input from a knowledgeable, caring professional can motivate us to do things for ourselves that we were not able to do on our own.

The question of when to seek professional help can be answered by looking over the following list of red flags.

Red flag feelings and behaviors that require immediate attention

• Inability to sleep.

• Feeling down, hopeless, or helpless most of the time.

• Concentration problems that are interfering with your work or home life.

• Using smoking, overeating, drugs, or alcohol to cope with difficult emotions.

• Negative or self-destructive thoughts or fears that you can't control.

• Thoughts of death or suicide.

If you identify with any of these red flag symptoms, make an appointment with a mental health professional - and the sooner, the better. It's much easier to overcome a mental or emotional problem if you deal with it while it's small, rather than waiting until it's a major, entrenched problem.

Emotional intelligence can help you strengthen your relationships, succeed at work, and overcome life's challenges.

The Wheel of Life

Wheel of Life

Finding balance in your life

When life is busy, or all your energy is focused on a special project, it's all too easy to find yourself "off balance", not paying enough attention to important areas of your life. While you need to have drive and focus if you're going to get things done, taking this too far can lead to frustration and intense PAIN. That's when it's time to take a "helicopter view" of your life, so that you can bring things back into balance.

This is where the Wheel of Life (or Life Wheel) can help. It helps you consider each area of your life in turn and assess what's off balance. And so, it helps you identify areas that need more attention. Figure 1 below shows an example wheel of life with example "dimensions" (we'll explain how to choose the right areas of life or dimensions for yourself below).

The Wheel of Life is powerful because it gives you a vivid visual representation of the way your life is currently, compared with the way you'd ideally like it to be. It is called the "Wheel of Life" because each area of your life is mapped on a circle, like the spoke of a wheel. Using the Tool Start by drawing a circle with the 6 areas pictured below and on a scale of 1-10 fill in the areas according to how you feel you are accomplished in these areas.

1. Start by brainstorming the 6 dimensions of your life that are important for you. Different approaches to this are: • The roles you play in life for example: husband/wife, father/mother, manager, colleague, team member, sports player, community leader, or friend; • Areas of life that are important to you for example: artistic expression, positive attitude, career, education, family, friends, financial freedom, physical challenge, pleasure, or public service; or • Your own combination of these (or different) things, reflecting the things that are your priorities in

life, you will find they fall into these 6 categories.

2. Write down these dimensions down on the Wheel of Life diagram, one on each spoke of the life wheel.

3. This approach assumes that you will be happy and fulfilled if you can find the right balance of attention for each of these dimensions. And different areas of your life will need different levels of attention at different times. So the next step is to assess the amount of attention you're currently devoting to each area.

Consider each dimension in turn, and on a scale of 1 (low) to 10 (high), write down the amount of attention you're devoting to that area of your life. Mark each score on the appropriate spoke of your Life Wheel.

4. Now join up the marks around the circle. Does your life wheel looked and feel balanced?

5. Next it's time to consider your ideal level in each area of your life. A balanced life does not mean getting 5 in each life area: some areas need more attention and focus than others at any time. And inevitably you will need to make choices and compromises, as your time and energy are not in unlimited supply!

So the question is, what would the ideal level of

attention be for you each life area?

Plot the "ideal" scores around your life wheel too.

6. Now you have a visual representation of your current life balance and your ideal life balance. What are the gaps? These are the areas of your life that need attention.

And remember that gaps can go both ways. There are almost certainly areas that are not getting as much attention as you'd like. However there may also be areas where you're putting in more effort than you'd ideally like. These areas are sapping energy and enthusiasm that may better be directed elsewhere.

7. Once you have identified the areas that need attention, it's time to plan the actions needed to work on regaining balance. Starting with the neglected areas, what things do you need to start doing to regain balance? In the areas that currently sap your energy and time, what can you STOP doing or reprioritize or delegate to someone else? Make a commitment to these actions by writing them on your worksheet of things you will start doing to move you in balance and things you will stop doing that are not serving you to achieve your balance.

8. Tip: You can use the Wheel of Life as preparation for goal setting. It helps identify the area you want to work on and is a great way of visualizing your current and desired life. Once you are working on improving your life balance, it's also a useful tool for monitoring how it changes over time.

The Wheel of Life is a great tool to help you improve your life balance. It helps you quickly and graphically identifies the areas in your life to which you want to devote more energy, and helps you understand where you might want to cut back.

The challenge now is to transform this knowledge and desire for a more balanced life into a positive program of action. Moving on Life and career coaching can be an incredibly powerful way of doing this. With the support of your own personal coach, you'll find it much easier to think through and maintain a positive program of change. Click here to find out more.

Forgiveness Will Set You Free

To live in gratitude one must live in forgiveness, Forgiveness Will Set You Free.

Forgiveness is greater than vengeance, compassion more powerful than Anger... another lesson I have learned over the years.

Forgiveness is a valuable gift that is neither easily obtained, nor easily given. Forgiveness is essential for life, forgiving others offers the gift that frees us of our past wrongs and and enables us to love with a renewed strength for the one we once felt wronged us.

Genuine forgiveness heals any hurts or wrongs. It strengthens the disheartened soul which has lost its way. It refreshes and renews our hope. It is through forgiveness that we are "born again" and "become like a child." In this way we regain the precious attitude of a willing mind which is ready to learn all over again.

The most intense conflicts, if overcome, leave behind a sense of security and calm that is not easily disturbed. It is just these intense conflicts and their conflagration which are needed to produce valuable and lasting results.

Even a happy life cannot be without a measure of darkness, and the word happy would lose its meaning if it were not balanced by sadness. It is far better to take things as they come along with patience and equanimity.

Thank you all for opening your hearts and sharing your triumphs, challenges and experiences with us. Let us all welcome each other and our new extended family here with blessing for the new year. Let us all take a moment today to pray in our own way for each others success in health, wealth and happiness keeping the needs of others above our own will bring forth paychecks of the heart money cannot replace. What will you share for us to pray for?

Dreams pass into the reality of action. From the actions stems the dream again; and this interdependence produces the highest form of living. Most people can look back over the years and identify a time and place at which their lives changed significantly. Whether by accident or design, these are the moments when, because of a readiness within us and a collaboration with events occurring around us, we are forced to seriously reappraise ourselves and the conditions under which we live and to make certain choices that will affect the rest of our lives. Gratitude is the key to success, forgiveness is the key to gratitude.

Pride of oneself and genuine love for others cannot coexist therefore one must give up what one cannot keep to get what one cannot lose... You have gifts that money cannot buy and treasures that can never be taken away, with that said forgiveness will set you free to live in fulfillment.

Science And Genetics Based On The Bible

Evidence

Creationists and evolutionists, Christians and non-Christians all have the *same* evidence—the same facts. Think about it: we all have the same earth, the same fossil layers, the same animals and plants, the same stars—the facts are all the same.

The difference is in the way we all *interpret* the facts. And why do we interpret facts differently? Because we start with different *presuppositions*. These are things that are assumed to be true, without being able to prove them. These then become the basis for other conclusions. *All* reasoning is based on presuppositions (also called *axioms*). This becomes especially relevant when dealing with past events.

Past and Present

We all exist in the present—and the facts all exist in the present. When one is trying to understand how the evidence came about (Where did the animals come from? How did the fossil layers form? etc.), what we are actually trying to do is to connect the past to the present.

However, if we weren't there in the past to observe events, how can we know what happened so we can explain the present? It would be great to have a time machine so we could know for sure about past events.

Christians of course claim they do, in a sense, have a "time machine." They have a book called the Bible that claims to be the Word of God who has always been there, and has revealed to us the major events of the past about which we need to know.

On the basis of these events (Creation, Fall, Flood, Babel, etc.), we have a set of presuppositions to build a way of thinking which enables us to interpret the evidence of the present.

Evolutionists have certain beliefs about the past/present that they presuppose, e.g. no God (or at least none who performed acts of special creation), so they build a different way of thinking to interpret the evidence of the present.

Thus, when Christians and non-Christians argue about the evidence, in reality they are arguing about their *interpretations* based on their *presuppositions*.

That's why the argument often turns into something like:

"Can't you see what I'm talking about?"

"No, I can't. Don't you see how wrong you are?"

"No, I'm not wrong. It's obvious that I'm right."

"No, it's not obvious." And so on.

These two people are arguing about the same evidence, but they are looking at the evidence through different glasses.

It's not until these two people recognize the

argument is really about the presuppositions they have to start with, that they will begin to deal with the foundational reasons for their different beliefs. A person will not interpret the evidence differently until they put on a different set of glasses—which means to change one's presuppositions.

I've found that a Christian who understands these things can actually put on the evolutionist's glasses (without accepting the presuppositions as true) and understand how they look at evidence. However, for a number of reasons, including spiritual ones, a non-Christian usually can't put on the Christian's glasses—unless they recognize the presuppositional nature of the battle and are thus beginning to question their own presuppositions.

It is of course sometimes possible that just by presenting "evidence," you can convince a person that a particular scientific argument for creation makes sense "on the facts." But usually, if that person then hears a different *interpretation* of the same evidence that seems better than yours, that person will swing away from your argument, thinking they have found "stronger facts."

However, if you had helped the person to understand this issue of presuppositions, then they will be better able to recognize this for what it is—a different interpretation based on differing presuppositions—i.e. starting beliefs.

As a teacher, I found that whenever I taught the students what I thought were the "facts" for creation, then their other teacher would just reinterpret the facts. The students would then come back to me saying, "Well Maam, you need to try again."

However, when I learned to teach my students how we interpret facts, and how interpretations are based on our presuppositions, then when the other teacher tried to reinterpret the facts, the students would challenge the teacher's basic assumptions. Then it wasn't the students who came back to me, but the other teacher! This teacher was upset with me because the students wouldn't accept her interpretation of the evidence and challenged the very basis of her thinking.

What was happening was that I had learned to teach the students *how* to think rather than just *what* to think. What a difference that made to my class! I have been overjoyed to find, sometimes decades later, some of those students telling me how they became active, solid Christians as a result.

Debate Terms

If one agrees to a discussion without using the Bible as some people insist, then *they* have set the terms of the debate. In essence these terms

are:

1. **“Facts” are neutral.** However, there are no such things as “brute facts;” *all* facts are interpreted. Once the Bible is eliminated in the argument, then the Christians’ presuppositions are gone, leaving them unable to effectively give an alternate interpretation of the facts. Their opponents then have the upper hand as they still have *their* presuppositions—see Naturalism, Logic and Reality.
2. **Truth can/should be determined independent of God.** However, the Bible states: ““The fear of the Lord is the beginning of wisdom”” (Psalm 111:10); ““The fear of the Lord is the beginning of knowledge”” (Proverbs 1:7). ““But the natural man does not receive the things of the Spirit of God, for they are foolishness to him; neither can he know them, because they are spiritually discerned”” (1 Corinthians 2:14).

A Christian cannot divorce the spiritual nature of the battle from the battle itself. A non-Christian is *not* neutral. The Bible makes this very clear: ““The one who is not with Me is against Me, and the one who does not gather with Me scatters”” (Matthew 12:30); ““And this is the condemnation, that the Light has come into the world, and men loved darkness rather than the Light, because their deeds were evil”” (John 3:19).

Agreeing to such terms of debate also implicitly accepts their proposition that the Bible’s account of the universe’s history is irrelevant to understanding that history!

Ultimately, God’s Word Convicts

1 Peter 3:15 and other passages make it clear we are to use every argument we can to convince people of the truth, and 2 Cor. 10:4–5 says we are to refute error (like Paul did in his ministry to the Gentiles). Nonetheless, we must never forget Hebrews 4:12: ““For the word of God is living and powerful and sharper than any two-edged sword, piercing even to the dividing apart of soul and spirit, and of the joints and marrow, and is a discerner of the thoughts and intents of the heart.”””

Also, Isaiah 55:11: ““So shall My word be, which goes out of My mouth; it shall not return to Me void, but it shall accomplish what I please, and it shall certainly do what I sent it to do.””

Even though our human arguments may be powerful, ultimately it is God’s Word that convicts and opens people to the truth. In all of our arguments, we must not divorce what we are saying from the Word that convicts.

Practical Application

When someone tells me they want “proof” or “evidence,” not the Bible, my response is as follows:

You might not believe the Bible but I do. And I believe it gives me the right basis to understand this universe and correctly interpret the facts around me. I'm going to give you some examples of how building my thinking on the Bible explains the world and is not contradicted by science. For instance, the Bible states that God made distinct *kinds* of animals and plants. Let me show you what happens when I build my thinking on this presupposition. I will illustrate how processes such as natural selection, genetic drift, etc. can be explained and interpreted. You will see how the science of genetics makes sense based upon the Bible.

One can of course do this with numerous scientific examples, showing how the issue of sin and judgment, for example, is relevant to geology and fossil evidence. And how the Fall of man, with the subsequent Curse on creation, makes sense of the evidence of harmful mutations, violence, and death.

Once I've explained some of this in detail, I then continue:

Now let me ask you to defend *your* position concerning these matters. Please show me how *your* way of thinking, based on *your* beliefs, makes sense of the same evidence. And I want you to point out where my science and logic are wrong.

In arguing this way, a Christian is:

1. Using biblical presuppositions to build a way of thinking to interpret the evidence.
2. Showing that the Bible and science go hand in hand.
3. Challenging the presuppositions of the other person (many are unaware they have these).
4. Forcing the debater to logically defend his position consistent with science and his own presuppositions (many will find that they cannot do this).
5. Honouring the Word of God that convicts the soul.

Remember, it's no good convincing people to believe in creation, without also leading them to believe and trust in the Creator/Redeemer, Jesus Christ. God honours those who honour His Word. We need to use God-honouring ways of reaching people with the truth of what life is all about.

Naturalism, Logic and Reality

Those arguing against creation may not even be conscious of their most basic presupposition, one which excludes God *a priori*, namely naturalism/materialism (everything came from matter, there is no supernatural, no prior creative intelligence). The following two real-life examples highlight some problems with that assumption:

1. A young man approached me at a seminar and

> stated, “Well, I still believe in the big bang, and that we arrived here by chance random processes. I don’t believe in God.” I answered him, “Well, then obviously your brain, and your thought processes, are also the product of randomness. So you don’t know whether it evolved the right way, or even what right would mean in that context. Young man, you don’t know if you’re making correct statements or even whether you’re asking me the right questions.”

The young man looked at me and blurted out, “What was that book you recommended?” He finally realized that his belief undercut its own foundations—such “reasoning” destroys the very basis for reason.

2. On another occasion, a man came to me after a seminar and said, “Actually, I’m an atheist. Because I don’t believe in God, I don’t believe in absolutes, so I recognize that I can’t even be sure of reality.” I responded, “Then how do you know you’re really here making this statement?” “Good point,” he replied. “What point?” I asked. The man looked at me, smiled, and said, “Maybe I should go home.” I stated, “Maybe it won’t be there.” “Good point,” the man said. “What point?” I replied.

This man certainly got the message. If there is no God, ultimately, philosophically, how can one talk about reality? How can one even rationally believe that there is such a thing as truth, let alone decide what it is?

Footnotes

1. In fact, science could avoid becoming still-born only in a Christian framework. Even secular philosophers of science are virtually unanimous on this. It required biblical presuppositions such as a real, objective universe, created by one Divine Lawgiver, who was neither fickle nor deceptive—and who also created the mind of man in a way that was *in principle* capable of understanding the universe.

2. This assumption is even defended, as a "practical necessity" in discussing scientific things *including origins*, by some professing Christians who are evolutionists.

This assumption is even defended, as a "practical necessity" in discussing scientific things *including origins*, by some professing Christians who are evolutionists.

The Most Common Road To Mediocrity Is Being Realistic

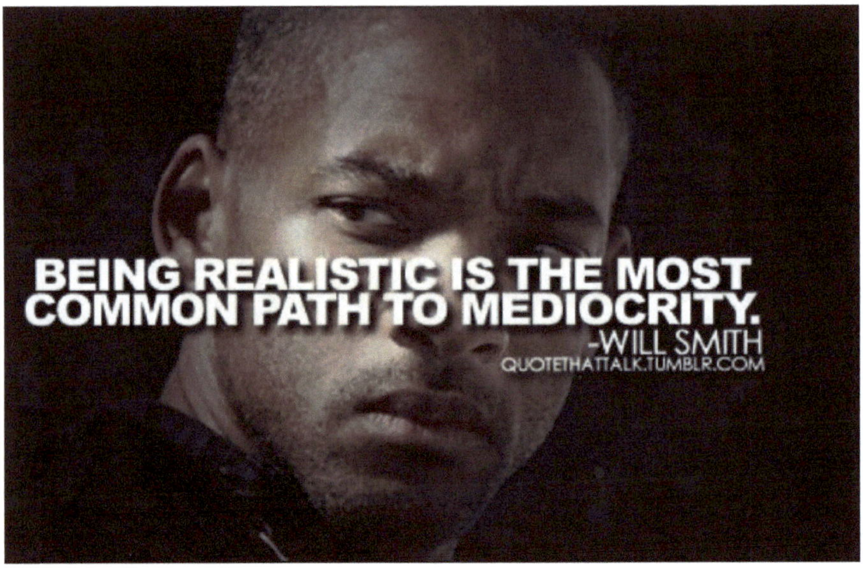

"The most common road to mediocrity is being realistic." - Will Smith

Ever notice something about realistic people?

... 90% of the time ... they're broke!

Realistic people can't stand change. Realistic people are usually cynical about change, paradigm shifts, new ideas and anything that clashes with their secure world. Realistic people will snear at you in the beginning ... but loose in the end. Realistic people stay stuck in a frame of mind that only exists in usually the past. Realistic people don't believe they can ever do anything other than what has already been done. Realistic people are mediocre at best.

Who wants to be realistic?

Let me tell you about *unrealistic* people. The people who make real differences in this world usually aren't tallying up the odds, and they aren't coming up with endless reasons why something can't work. They don't care what's realistic. Let me ask you a question, what the hell in this world is realistic? We wake up every day and do things people would have thought were impossible 20-30 years ago. What if you tried to explain the Internet to someone in 1985? You'd probably have been told your brains are fried. Unrealistic things are happening every day. And if you think being realistic is going to create the kind of life you want, you're sadly mistaken. Even though things are changing so rapidly every day, we still have the time to sit back and decide what is realistic and what's not. BS! There is no such thing as realistic and there is no such a thing as unrealistic. The only thing that doesn't change is your belief of what is "suppose" to happen. Only you can change that.

"The 95% of realistic people in this world work

for the 5% of unrealistic people." - Will Smith

The unrealistic people rule the world. Is it realistic to be the chairman of a top Fortune 500 company? Is it realistic to train your whole life to win a gold medal? Is Open Source software outperforming technology giants realistic? It's scary to think what the world would be like if some of the great inventors of our time would have been realistic people, who payed close attention to the odds against them. We blame this stuff on luck, or someone who had a fluke opportunity. Even success-minded people fall into this trap. But a few of us know this: **when you think unrealistically, it opens a new space in your mind that didn't exist there before, a higher level of thinking.** Albert Einstein said that **"a problem can't be solved at the same level of thinking that it was made at."**

Here's a question to ask yourself: **Am I realistic and in what situations am I realistic?** Make sure you pay close attention to the answers you give yourself.

Next time someone tells you something is unrealistic, your answer should be ... "Compared to what?"

A good belief to instill in yourself is that nothing is impossible if you really want it bad enough and do whatever it takes. Maybe it takes working late

and starting early, a sickening work ethic, relentless repetition until it works. Just take someone who has accomplished something, that you would consider, nearly impossible and use them as a role model. What makes your little challenges so hard to defeat? Are you even giving 10% of what you could?

Success, What Is Your Definition?

It's More Important To Be Happy Than To Be Rich
By

Here's the opening paragraph from my forthcoming book, *Financial Fertility: Your Missing Money Link*. It's the sum of everything

I've learned during my five year journey to get rich slowly:

You don't want to be rich; you want what you believe the money will buy you to make you happy. Many people mistakenly believe that the former leads to the latter. While it's certainly true that money can help you achieve your goals, provide for your future, and make life more enjoyable, merely having money doesn't guarantee happiness.

Many of us (including me) get wrapped up in the belief that having more money is the key to a better life. It's not, the key to a better life is increased happiness. For some people, that does mean more money. But according to the research Tal Ben-Shahar shares in his book Happier, most of us would be better served by:

Creating rituals around the things we love to do.

Expressing gratitude for the good things in our lives.

Setting meaningful goals that reflect our values and interests.

Playing to our strengths instead of dwelling on weaknesses.

Simplifying our lives, not just the Stuff, the time.

We're more likely to lead happy lives by putting these principles into practice than by getting another raise at work, especially if the increased income would only lead to increased spending. When we focus on monetary goals, we run the risk of becoming trapped on the "hedonic treadmill" (also known as lifestyle inflation), working harder and harder to make more and more money. This does not lead to happiness.

Sometimes money can buy happiness

Wealth and happiness aren't mutually exclusive, of course. According to financial writer Jonathan Clements, financial stability improves your well-being in three ways:

If you have money, you don't have to worry about it. By living below your means, you can obtain a degree of financial control even if you aren't rich. Avoiding debt gives you options.

Money can give you the freedom to pursue your passions. What is it you want out of life? What gives you a sense of purpose? These are the sorts of things you want to pursue in retirement. Better yet, try to structure your career around something you love to do.

Money can buy you time with friends and family.

In fact, Clements says, true wealth comes from relationships, not from dollars and cents. Social capital is worth more than financial capital.

Money is a tool. As with any tool, a skilled craftsman can use it to build something amazing: a meaningful life filled with family and friends. If you're not careful, if you don't have a plan, the life you construct with your money can be a tenuous thing, even dangerous.

Lessons learned

Studies show that the pursuit of money is less likely to bring personal fulfillment than focusing on self-improvement and, especially, close relationships with others. Here are a handful of lessons I've learned during my research into the connection between money and wealth. I didn't come up with any of these ideas; they're products of actual research into what makes us happy:

People who are materialistic tend to be less happy than those who aren't. If your aim is to have more money and more Stuff, you'll be less content than others whose goals are built around relationships or mental/spiritual fulfillment. (Life will pay you what you ask of it.)

Over saving does not lead to happiness. While it's important to save for the future (and to cope with current emergencies), research shows that over saving can actually have a negative impact on your quality of life. If you're meeting your goals for saving, it's okay to spend some on the things that make you happy.

Experiences tend to make us happier than material things. We have different reactions to the money we spend on experiences and the money we spend on Stuff: When we spend on experiences, our perceptions are magnified (meaning we feel happier or sadder than when we spend on Stuff), and the feelings tend to linger longer. And since most of our experiences are positive, spending on activities instead of material goods generally makes us happier.

When we lower our expectations, our happiness increases. High expectations come when we compare ourselves to others or when advertising bombards us. We come to accept the things we see on TV as "normal", and because we don't have these things, we feel inadequate.

Our expectations rise, and before long we're caught up in lifestyle inflation. If we can consciously manage our expectations, both financial and otherwise we increase our sense of well-being.

Really, there's only one-way to ever be satisfied with how much money you have: You must define how much is enough. True happiness comes when you learn to be content with what you have. If you don't take the time to figure out what enough means to you, you'll always be unhappy with your financial situation.

How much is enough?

Enough looks different to each of us. It's not just different amounts of money, but different types of wealth. For me, enough is being debt free with the time freedom to travel the world to participate in the many bicycle events and to train in different environments to enrich my experience of cycling. For you, enough may mean living in a small apartment but owning a boat and having the freedom to sail for months at a time.

To find enough, you have to set goals. You have to look inside to find your morals, values and beliefs that make up your blueprint. It can take months or years to get clear on what makes a meaningful life for you, or it can take a moment to find clarity, once you've done this, you can make choices that reflect your priorities.

After all, that's why you're doing this. You're not building wealth just so you can bathe in buckets of cash. You're building wealth so you don't have to worry about money, so you can pursue your passions, and so you can spend time with your family and friends.

Remember, my friends: True wealth isn't about money. True wealth is about relationships, about good health, and about continued self-improvement. True wealth is about happiness. Ultimately, it's more important to be happy than it is to be rich because success without fulfillment is failure.

Cerebral Nudity Exposed

A proven methodology to trick your brain into thinking you're happy

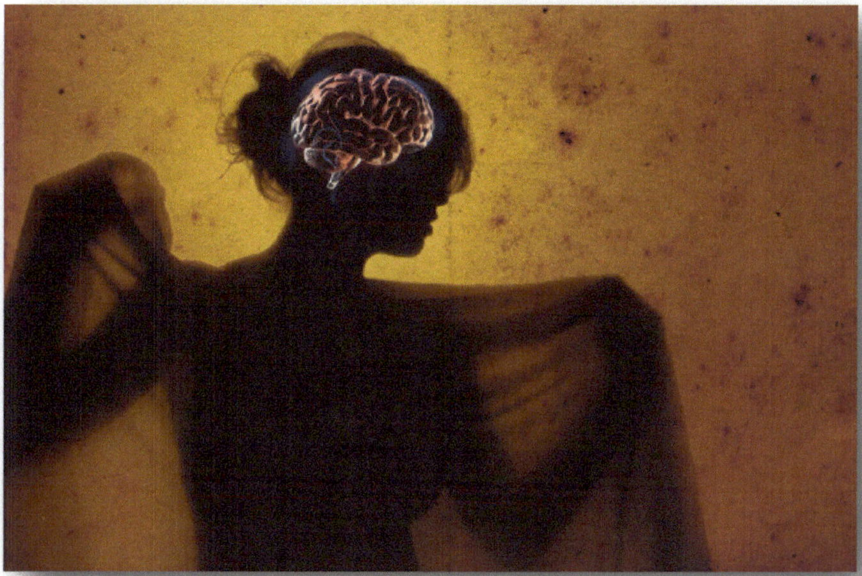

I'm going to get right to the point because I want YOU to be genuinely happy: smile, relax, sit up straight. You're welcome.

In case you're interested, here's a little more context. Scientists have known for a long time that emotions are accompanied by numerous changes in the body, from elevation in the heart rate to flexion of the zygomatic major muscle (i.e. smiling). However, we've come to understand more recently that it's a two way street. Your brain actually pays attention to what your body is doing, and it affects your emotions. This was first called the "facial feedback hypothesis", but it applies to more than just muscles of the face. The good news is that while it's sometimes hard to control our emotions, it's much easier to control our muscles. So to teach you how to use your body to trick your brain, I am releasing a series of quick tips for boosting your happiness, tranquility and confidence.

Quick Tip For Happiness:

Smile. Seriously, just do it. You'll even enjoy this post more if you do. (If you're thinking "I'm not doing that, I don't want to enjoy this post more" then feel free to stop reading). Your smile is a powerful tool. Most people think that we smile because we feel happy, but it can go the other way as well: we feel happy because we smile.

One of the best experiments to demonstrate this came from the late '80s. The researchers did not want to influence the results by telling subjects that the study was about emotion, so they devised an ingenious way to get the subjects to flex certain muscles of their face without knowing why. They had subjects hold a pencil in one of three ways. The first group held the pencil widthwise between their teeth, forcing a smile. The second group held the pencil in their lips lengthwise, which means they couldn't smile, and were actually making kind of a frown. The control group held the pencil in their hand. Then the subjects looked at some cartoons, and rated how funny they were. The "smile" group gave the cartoons much higher "funny" ratings than the "frown" group, while the control group was somewhere in the middle.

In a more recent study, subjects were presented with a series of faces, which had happy, neutral or angry expressions. The subjects were told that the study was attempting to measure reaction time of facial muscles, but they were really studying emotion. Regardless of the image, subjects were instructed to either "raise their cheeks" (aka smile) or "contract their eyebrows" (aka frown). The instructed facial expression influenced how the images were perceived. When subjects smiled they found the images more pleasant than when they frowned. On top of that, the effects of the brief smile even persisted 4 minutes later.

Facial feedback works because the brain senses the flexion of certain facial muscles (like the zygomatic major, which is required to smile) and interprets it as "Oh I must be happy about something." Similarly, if that muscle isn't flexed then your brain thinks, "Oh, I must not be happy".

In addition to the direct neural feedback, in the real world you also get the added advantage of social feedback. Smiles are infectious (perhaps another post on mirror neurons in the future). So even if you don't feel much happier, the people around you are more likely to smile, and that can improve your mood as well.

Lastly, if you can work up the energy to actually smile, you'll probably have an even bigger benefit. While the zygomatic major controls the corners of your mouth, there is a muscle at the corner of the eyes called the orbicularis oculi that only flexes when you're actually smiling. So if you really want to get the biggest facial feedback benefit, find something to laugh about (perhaps the fact that you're trying to flex certain muscles to trick your brain into thinking you're happy). That will likely generate a true smile. This is also a great tip for becoming more photogenic (trust me, I mean look at that profile pic). The reason many people think their smiles look fake in pictures is that their smiles are fake. The corners of their eyes are not flexed.

So next time you want to improve your mood a little, all you have to do is flex your zygomatic major muscles to raise the corners of your mouth.

Leading An Authentic Life

Discover your full potential, to create a better world share your knowledge.

Who do you think you are?

Most of us have an idea of who we are, how we feel, how we behave socially and also, how we are deep down inside. We play roles within our family, at work, at play, and in our community. We have our secret hearts, the way we think we are that no one else knows, the way we wish we were and the ways that we fear we are.

Who you think you are has a lot to do with your original DNA programming and who you really are at your Core has nothing to do with your original DNA programming.

What creates this dichotomy? Well, it is true that we come in with ½ of our DNA from our mother and ½ from our father and along with that is our ancestral DNA and added to that is the information we receive as we develop in the womb and beyond.

What we know now (and the Human Genome Study demonstrated this) is that the DNA we bring in with us is just the start. It is a core set of programs that can have a profound effect on how you make decisions and how you view yourself, your unconscious beliefs, and what feels 'right' to you in the world.

However, due to research by such scientific luminaries as Cell Biologist, Dr. Bruce Lipton, we know that many of your DNA programs are epigenetically created. In other words, new DNA programs are created by information coming into the cells from the outside, from your thoughts, your experiences and even your deliberate intentions.

Where it was once thought that you come in to this world as a fully-formed being, with all of your beliefs and behaviors and capabilities and identity set in stone and immutable; we know now that you are changing all the time, either consciously or unconsciously, or both.

You have the capacity to change your

blueprint, who you are, how you view the world, and how you want to Be in the world at any given moment.

I use The One Command to make my changes, along with awareness work and consciousness work and play, letting go, and re-creating. What do you use to make the changes you want in your life? It is a good idea to sort that out and create a plan for yourself, to choose a new version of yourself that will fulfill your need to be renewed.

A starting point is to begin from some of your original behavioral programs, your own Behavioral DNA. There are many styles of behavior and they often fit into 4 basic categories that serve as a model for how you Behave and how you view the world, how you make decisions, choose what serves you, and even how you make choices.

These programs also influence how you perceive the world around you, including other peoples behavior and your perceptions of what their behavior means to you.

There are even models of the patterns, the one I work with includes a simple approach to looking at your core DNA programs, those unconscious behaviors that influence you so deeply in your view of the world at large and your place in it. You have the capacity to then take that awareness and choose your own new way of being in the world from a new perspective.

This information gives you guidelines to work from so that you can release the behaviors and beliefs that aren't working for you and replace them with the thoughts, actions and beliefs about the world and your place in it that are fulfilling for you.

When I work with clients we use a model with category names and background information and guidelines to use or change the behaviors and ideas and beliefs that work or don't work in their lives. So lets take some pieces of that information that you can use to decide what programs in you may be living from.

Are you by nature a person who is very direct and straightforward, a person who speaks your mind fairly easily, takes charge when necessary and tends to keep your private life private?

If so, it is likely that these behaviors have served you well as long as you have also developed your capacity to listen well to others and take their ideas and feelings into consideration, to open your heart to those closest to you and to allow yourself to play a little.

Are you by nature a person who is often called a visionary, a person who tends to be very social and outgoing (but often feels shy inside and has a need to retreat into yourself sometimes), a person who has a million great ideas and shifts gears very easily?

If so, it is likely that people love to be in relationship with you, until they don't. It may serve you well to develop your innate compassion into a higher level of listening to and attending to others closest to you in your life. There is a saying about this particular pattern of behavior, Well, enough about me, what do You think about me?

You are charming and charismatic and it may serve you well to truly open yourself up to the vulnerability of a deeper connection to others - you have that capacity inside, and you are truly loving, let go!

Are you by nature a person who loves to know how things work, how things fit together, what patterns show up in life and nature, do you know exactly what Fibonacci Numbers and The Golden Section are in nature, and do you care?

You are often quite brilliant, very curious about many things or at least about everything in one area. You can be very focused on your project or work and you often prefer to work alone, master of your own environment.

Where you might choose to expand is in your willingness to let others into your world, to go beyond the walls of your home and office and open to more variety of experience in your life.

You are a great family person, in fact your family can be the major part of your world other than your work. Where you can gain even more from life is by being a greater part of your community.

Are you by nature a person whose nature is focused more on others than yourself? Are you known for your compassion and caring and helpfulness and kindness? These are all obviously great things to do and great ways to be.

Where you can decide to expand your experience of life is to offer yourself that same level of compassion, caring, helpfulness, kindness and respect to yourself. You also get to choose to have fun just for the sake of it, and take that 'Sunday best' outfit out of the closet and start wearing it anytime you want.

Break a few rules, not the ones about speed limits and not Texting while driving, but the rules you carry inside about loving yourself as much as you love others, attending to your own needs, and speaking your truth always, knowing it is ok and you will still be loved and accepted.

Who do you want to be?

So you can see, this is just the tip of the iceberg

of Behavioral DNA patterns that reside in the Core of who you are and with a little appreciation of those patterns and a little awareness of how these patterns shape your view of the world, how you make choices, how you process information and how you behave toward yourself and others, you can use those core patterns as a starting point and then refine them into just the person you have always wanted to be.

Information is freedom, you are here reading this because you are choosing to expand your knowledge and expand you life, that is also a Behavioral DNA pattern and it is a pattern that will continue to serve you well. Live and Learn.

Love & Money: Is There Balance In Your Relationship?

If there is strain and stress now what could it be like if and when there is a major windfall? It may not always be the lack of money but the control of it or something else. Hopefully this will shed a little light and give you some things to consider.

Do your finances cause tension in your relationship?

Many relationships face intense stress and anxiety over money issues. It seems that love and money have an important connection with couples.

Perhaps your current relationship is feeling the impact of this connection now. How would you rate your relationship on a 1-10 love and money scale, where one is how loving and passionate your connection is and ten is the degree to which you have mastered your money concerns?

For instance: a 10/10 would be the best of everything; you're in intimate love and ecstatic passion with one another and you feel absolute financial certainty and freedom (where you don't ever have to work, unless you want to, and you never have to worry about your bills being paid, since the returns from your secure and growing investments easily cover any expenses you could have).

In many ways, we trade our life energy for money. So, we need to respect what goes into making, protecting and enjoying money. What it can do for others and us in the way of convenience, creativity and contribution is truly expansive. So, what if I told you there are ways to improve in both love and money simultaneously?

What makes us happy? Pleasure, right? (At least over the short-term) Progress is what really makes us feel happy over the long term. In the love and money game of life, we have both practical and emotionally driven needs that must be met at high levels in order for us to feel like we are joyfully winning in a satisfying way. So, we shall look at both.

To achieve progress in finances and relationships,

you must honestly know where you are, get clear about where you want to be and close the gap between the two step-by-step. Removing what's in the way, designing a workable plan and taking proven action to hit your target reduces the gap.

Let's take a look at what could be obstructing your passion and pocketbook, how to remove it and how to use proven strategies that can realign your relationship with satisfying love and financial progress. Notice that love comes first because success without fulfillment is failure.

Everyone has the emotional need for certainty, but one person in a relationship may be more predominantly driven than the other. How much of what you do, don't do or get anxious about stems from your need to feel comfortable or stable?

Your need for certainty may be why you don't change jobs, why you eat unhealthy "comfort" food, procrastinate or watch way too much TV, none of which may be helping your bank account most effectively.

Each of us has different vehicles through which we meet our need for certainty. One may feel comfort from having a savings or retirement account; another may need to feel safe by having a particular level of income or type of job stability.

Knowing what you and your partner need to feel comfortable is vital, because when you don't feel certain enough, fear can dominate you and your passion will go out the window. Compassion Facilitates Forgiveness

Fear can bring difficulty to your communication, create disconnection and threaten the very stability of your relationship. You may think, "This jerk doesn't know how to communicate," when in fact, it may just be that he's afraid. Understanding this can empower you to respond from compassion instead of reacting un-resourcefully. Remember the meaning of respond is the ability to respond.

Together you will be in a better position to receive ideas, change perceptions and take necessary or inspired action. As you do, watch how obstructing fears subside, passion increases and creative ideas to improve your finances get enacted.

Each of us also has a need for loving connection, yet one partner could need this even more than their partner needs certainty. "We could be broke, but if I know we still love each other, I'll be fine." Sounds good on paper, but if the partner who has a dominant need for certainty feels out of control economically and thus withdraws affections, the relationship could become stressed to a breaking point over time.

One key to navigating such a love/money challenge is to seek to unselfishly give your partner what they most need, and to do it in a way that resonates with them. For example, provide the certainty they need by telling your mate that you will always be there for them and that you believe they have what it takes to work through their financial trials.

In another other case, you might offer love and connection to your significant other by getting out of your self-concern and giving them words of kindness, physical affection, thoughtful care and supportive actions.

While this may not seem like it has much to do with money, consider the fact that studies have shown that sharing a passionate kiss with one's honey before leaving for work has a considerable positive impact on the annual income of that household.

Having first sought to understand and meet your partner's needs, it is also important to openly communicate what you need most, and it may be appropriate to ask for the help from both your partner and others. Partners that work together well can overcome huge things financially. In fact, abundance is ever-present.

You just need to access it through positive expectation, willingness to bring unexpected and enthusiastic value to others (in ways that make them want more) and massive action using feedback along the way.

6 Ways to Thrive in Tough Times

Tough times can bring you to your knees more important if you embrace it they can also raise you to new heights.

You can be stressed to the max on a bad day, yet, as long as life seems manageable, you don't usually look for new strategies to get through it. The tendency is to pick yourself, dust yourself off, grit your teeth and keep on going, the important thing to remember when this happens is that if you keep doing what you've always done you will keep getting what you've always gotten. I call this insanity because doing what you've always done expecting a different result is insanity. During prolonged or sudden tough times, normal defense mechanisms are not enough to keep you from feeling vulnerable and overwhelmed.

It's when events feel overwhelmingly beyond your control that one of two things will happen, you will either find new ways to cope or are pulled down by the undertow. Your usual defenses are inadequate to protect you from overwhelming long-term stress. Stress can build gradually beyond tolerance level, or a surprising turn of events like those recently reported in the news can create the kind of vulnerability that demands openness to change.

The soft inner core of your being feels exposed. This exposure opens a crack in the old armor through which an opportunity for renewed life can shine.

Here are six tips that can help you thrive in tough times.

Nourish Yourself

break free and break through to acknowledge your stress and be kind to yourself. What nourishes you, inspirational reading, music, a cup of tea in a warm bath? Are there people or places, a favorite chair or spot in nature that provide sustenance? Make nurturing yourself every day a priority.

Stay Present

See things better than they are. Take life one day, one moment at a time. Tough times are more manageable when you pay attention to making decisions and taking action on only the next step. Fearful preoccupation or worries about dire imagined future of possibilities can leave you open to illness, accidents and errors in judgment that compound your problems. Scale down, simplify your activities and concentrate your precious energy supply on only what is critically important right now.

Accept Support

This can be difficult for people who prize self-sufficiency. Remember it is as virtuous to receive, as it is to give. Without the receiver, the giver has no way to share their abundant gifts. Don't deprive your friends and family of the pleasure to help you when you need it. Shared burdens provide opportunities for enhanced closeness and appreciation for one another.

Trust Your Resilience

Chances are you have been through tough times before. What natural strengths did you rely upon in those situations? How did you make it through adolescence, childbirth, marriage, divorce, school, your first job? What are your natural inner resources? Trust that you have what you need to see this tough time through because all that you need is within you.

Visualize Success – See yourself moving into a new chapter of life. How do you want to write that chapter? Creation begins in the imagination. If you can think it, you can create it. In order to be free to dream and hope for something new, you must let go of old visions, descriptions and limitations of the person you think you are and you will become the person your are meant to be because If you talk about it, it's a dream, if you envision it, it's possible, but if **you schedule it, it's real**.

Forgive Past Errors

Forgive past hurts, and people who may have inflicted them, knowingly or unknowingly. This is not out of kindness to them, rather out of kindness to yourself. After all, you are the one carrying the burden of these hurts. Forgive yourself for mistakes or paths not taken. Release the burden of the past so you can travel lighter in the present.

In times of crisis and radical change, remember that living means growing. I have never seen anything in nature grow backward. So, as bad as you feel, and as much as you doubt it, if you are alive you are growing.

Growth is creative. So, take advantage of the opportunity in these tough times to re-create your life by nourishing yourself, staying present, accepting support, trusting your resilience, visioning possibilities and letting go of the past and perceived limitations.

Even though tough times are hard, they can also be the best times to explore ways to live more harmoniously with yourself and others. Always find opportunities in each challenge.

Psychology Changes Physiology

I am sure many have heard that it has been said many times it's a woman's prerogative to change her mind - well little did we realize maybe how important it is and how much a change in thought and a change in word can change everything - even our health - I hope you will read and think about the points here.

Changing Your Mind:

Developing A Wellness Attitude the Easy Way

How important do you think an attitude is when it comes to health and longevity? What exactly is an attitude and does it sub-divide into smaller parts of one larger overall state? Is your attitude sabotaging your ambitions? Can attitude alone cause illness and dis-ease?

The bottom line answer to all of the above is attitude can be everything when it comes to wellness. Most think of a positive attitude as having something significant to say about success or prosperity or even relationships, but these same people often fail to recognize just how important attitude is when it comes to health and longevity.

Yet, if you simply search the Internet or read your paper, or follow the news, and so on, you discover that every day we are being informed of the powerful effect attitude has on wellness. Not directly so much as indirectly and even subliminally.

Think of the issues we see reported as the primary causes underlying so much illness today. Repeatedly we hear of addictions, obesity, fast food, various food additives, fitness and more. How important do you think attitude, a reflection of our beliefs, is to matters of this sort.

There is no denying the importance of remaining fit as a part and parcel of good health. Indeed, in almost all areas of health care, exercise is emphasized as both a measure for full recovery and as a prophylactic preventing future illness. With that said, most Americans fail when it comes to a regular exercise habit or routine.

The Center for Disease Control (CDC) considers exercise a key to good health. In their February 2011 report, they laid out what was necessary to curb the rising obesity problem and reduce the cost of medical care and prescription drugs.

"In a checkup of the nation's health, the CDC found that fewer than two in 10 Americans get the recommended levels of exercise, and more than a quarter of U.S. adults do not devote any time to physical activity."

The cost involved as a result of the lack of exercise on health is devastating as is the out of pocket dollar cost. Indeed, according to the 2011 government numbers, "34 percent of American adults are obese and another 34 percent are overweight.

Obese individuals spend on average 40 percent more on health care every year compared with individuals of normal weight. While exercise is nearly free, obesity-related health care costs total an estimated $147 billion annually. The cost of treating diabetes totals some $116 billion. (Federal guidelines call for 150 minutes of moderate to vigorous physical activity every week, including two days of full-body strengthening."

Managing our personal health care involves much more than just attentiveness to a regular exercise regime. It also includes nutrition, rest, stress management, and attitude. Now matters of nutrition are obvious and the need for proper sleep and stress reduction are also well known.

That said, many people fail to do anything about stress. That is, we know when we're not sleeping well and therefore typically take action to mitigate sleeplessness. However, stress builds slowly, accumulating over time.

There are two inherent aspects of stress then that we need to be cognizant of. The first, stress does accumulate and can manifest suddenly through many disease routes, perhaps the best known of which is cardiac disease. It can wreak havoc on the optimal operation of our endocrine, immune, and autonomic nervous system. Second, stress can manifest slowly by way of tensions, anxiety, blood pressure and so forth.

Many people find that they assuage anxiety and

stress by eating or smoking. So, all the while stress is accumulating it may be taking another path that is further damaging one's health.

Living long and remaining healthy is something we all want. Ask the teenager if they would like to live to be 100 and the likely answer is an emphatic "No." Unfortunately that is due to their expectation or attitude toward age and "old" people.

All too often aging takes a toll that betrays our best and instead reveals the lack of attention we gave to our health when we were younger and had it. This is the image that so many young people see and this is the image that they therefore put in their heads as the expectation for what will happen to them when they too grow old.

Thus the statement, "Only the brave grow old." Now, ask a 99 year old if he/she wishes to live to be 100 and the answer is typically yes! So what's the lesson here?

There are at least two levels to be considered with regard to expectation or attitude. The first comes down to the fact that the hard research shows that our expectations often come true.

Consider this by way of example. Years ago, I did some research regarding the role of the mind in wellness, and it eventually led to a CD training collection and companion book: Wellness: Mind Over Matter. One of the studies I came across was most interesting and relevant to the whole matter of my beliefs regarding aging and, for that matter, dying.

In this case, the Chinese birth sign was used to compare death with the expectation factor. According to the Chinese system of astrology, each birth sign provides information about the individual in terms of their occupational proclivities, talents, interests, and even the eventual cause of death.

According to researcher David Phillips, the data showed a clear relationship between the astrological sign and the cause of death. In other words, if you were born believing that you would die of cancer due to astrology, then cancer is what you got.

Attitude is part and parcel of expectation. Our attitude influences us on a daily basis. When our mood is down our body bears witness to it. It's no wonder people approach us and ask, "What's wrong?" when we feeling blue.

Our attitudes are telegraphed by our facial expressions, our body posture, tension and other physical characteristics as we go through life. Let me remind you that the body analogously has two budgets, one for growth and one for defense.

When we keep the body in a state of vigilance, anxious or angry, sad or blaming, and so forth, we essentially spend our budget on defense. The body pays a very real price for this!

Maintaining an optimistic and positive attitude then becomes as important to our health as exercise and diet. Our attitude definitely impacts what we find stressful and how we desensitize stressful stimuli. Our attitude also directly influences our sleeping patterns.

From an overall perspective, we must understand that it is the thoughts in our head, our attitude if you will, that determines much of our health. With the proper attitude, we find exercise fun and rewarding.

With a healthy outlook on life, we enjoy good nutrition and pass on the fast foods and fattening sweets. With an optimistic attitude we have every right to expect a long healthy life full of smiles and laughter. With the right attitude we find sleep easy and natural at days end. With an attitude of respect and love toward ourselves, we find our body remains young, fit and healthy!

Self-sabotage exists because of a belief. Our attitudes are mirrors, tiny examples of our beliefs. Our beliefs are intricately connected like spider silk forming a giant web–they do not exist in isolation. Touch any one belief and the entire web is disturbed and this can be why it seems so difficult sometimes to make a change.

That said, new research confirms that of all the things a person can do to improve the quality of their life, nothing is as powerful as a personality change, but making this change unaided can be challenging to say the least.

Seeds Of Life, Seeds Of Success

Seeds of Life

the gift of a new beginning

A successful businessman was growing old and knew it was time to choose a successor to take over the business.

Instead of choosing one of his Directors or his children, he decided to do something different. He called all the young executives in his company together because by realizing that one's character is defined by what we do when we think no one is looking he was motivated to choose this process of promotion.

He said, "It is time for me to step down and choose the next CEO. I have decided to choose one of you. “The young executives were Shocked, but the boss continued. “I am going to give each one of you a SEED today - one very special SEED. I want you to plant the seed, water it, and come back here one year from today with what you have grown from the seed I have given you.

I will then judge the plants that you bring, and the one I choose will be the next CEO.”

One man, named Jim, was there that day and he, like the others, received a seed. He went home and excitedly, told his wife the story. She helped him get a pot, soil and compost and he planted the seed. Everyday, he would water it and watch to see if it had grown. After about three weeks, some of the other executives began to talk about their seeds and the plants that were beginning to grow.

Jim kept checking his seed, but nothing ever grew. Three weeks, four weeks, five weeks went by, still nothing.

By now, others were talking about their plants, Jim didn’t have a plant and he felt like a failure.

Six months went by — still nothing in Jim’s pot. He just knew he had killed his seed. Everyone else had trees and tall plants, but he had nothing

Jim didn’t say anything to his colleagues,

however, he just kept watering and fertilizing the soil – He so wanted the seed to grow. A year finally went by and all the young executives of the company brought their plants to the CEO for inspection.

Jim told his wife that he wasn't going to take an empty pot. But she asked him to be honest about what happened. Jim felt sick to his stomach, it was going to be the most embarrassing moment of his life, but he knew his wife was right. He took his empty pot to the boardroom.

When Jim arrived, he was amazed at the variety of plants grown by the other executives. They were beautiful – in all shapes and sizes. Jim put his empty pot on the floor and many of his colleagues laughed, a few felt sorry for him!

When the CEO arrived, he surveyed the room and greeted his young executives.

Jim just tried to hide in the back. "My, what great plants, trees and flowers you have grown," said the CEO. "Today one of you will be appointed the next CEO!"

All of a sudden, the CEO spotted Jim at the back of the room with his empty pot. He ordered the Financial Director to bring him to the front. Jim was terrified.. He thought, "The CEO knows I'm a failure! Maybe he will have me fired!"

When Jim got to the front, the CEO asked him what had happened to his seed, Jim told him the story.

The CEO asked everyone to sit down except Jim. He looked at Jim, and then announced to the young executives, “Behold your next Chief Executive Officer!

His name is “Jim!” Jim couldn’t believe it. Jim couldn’t even grow his seed.

“How could he be the new CEO?” the others said.

Then the CEO said, “One year ago today, I gave everyone in this room a seed. I told you to take the seed, plant it, water it, and bring it back to me today. But I gave you all boiled seeds; they were dead - it was not possible for them to grow.

All of you, except Jim, have brought me trees and plants and flowers. When you found that the seed would not grow, you substituted another seed for the one I gave you. Jim was the only one with the courage and honesty to bring me a pot with my seed in it. Therefore, he is the one who will be the new Chief Executive Officer!”

* If you plant honesty, you will reap trust

* If you plant goodness, you will reap friends

* If you plant humility, you will reap greatness

* If you plant perseverance, you will reap contentment

* If you plant consideration, you will reap perspective

* If you plant hard work, you will reap success

* If you plant forgiveness, you will reap reconciliation

So, be careful what you plant now; it will determine what you will reap later.

Anger is Danger = Side Effects

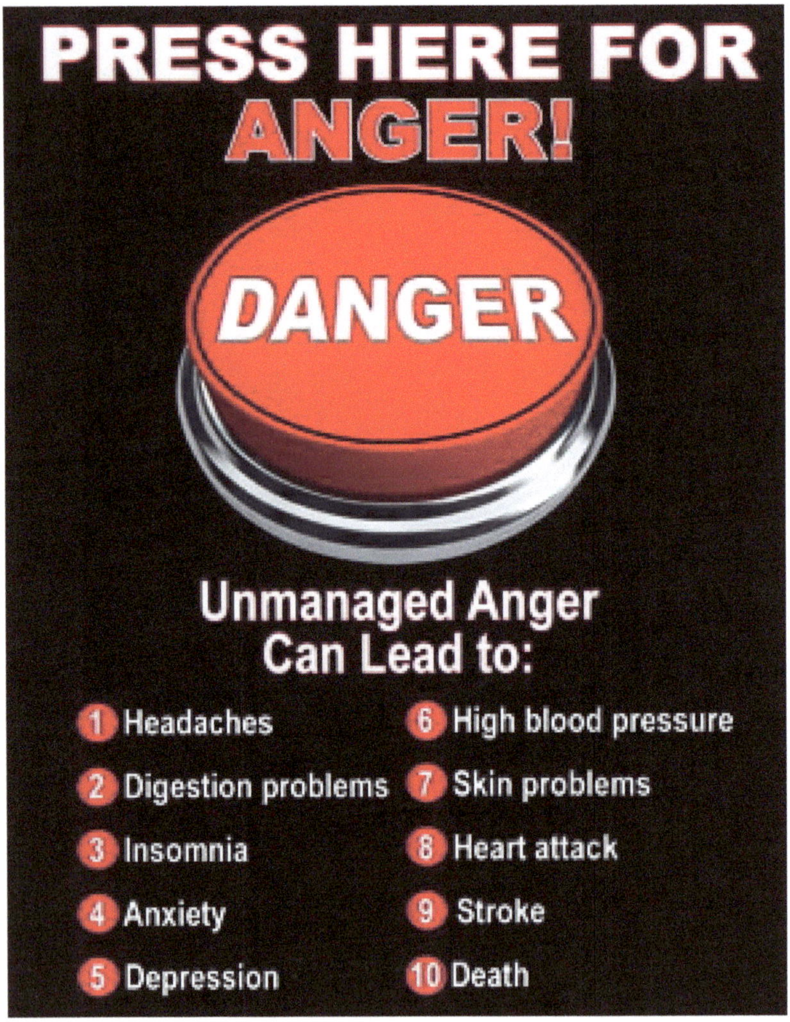

Anger is a human emotion characterized by a strong feeling of displeasure and hostility, precipitated by real or supposed grievances or insults. Like any other emotion, anger is also accompanied by physiological and biological changes. The heart rate and the blood pressure goes up and there is increased discharge of energy hormones such as adrenaline and nor-adrenaline. Changing lifestyle, increasing workload, uncertainty about fate of jobs and organizations; all these are causing stress, worry and anger in today's work force.

According to Kassinove and his colleague, a study in 1997 revealed, 58% of anger episode included yelling and screaming while less than 10% involved physical aggression. Sometimes anger can be normal and helpful, but this is a very small percentage.

The most common sensations of anger are a tight feeling in the upper chest, flush of warmth in the face and the upper body and the tightening of the jaw. Take a few minutes and try to find out what sensations you feel when you are angry. It is important that you admit to yourself, even if you feel slightest of anger, if you want to improve your life.

Cost of Anger: Often one has to pay a heavy cost for anger. It could result in irrational thinking, could disrupt team performance or could result in decreased motivation levels. Repressed anger is even worse as it could erupt any time and cause irreversible damage. Angry individuals have 3 times higher risk of heart attack if below the age of 55 years and 6 times if above the age of 55 years.

Cause of Anger: Following situation can be responsible for " triggering " anger in a person where he/she may find it difficult to exercise patience.

3. When a person is extremely stressed out, facing difficulties or when things are not moving as expected.
4. Disappointment at not being able to fulfill expectations, either self-expectations or that of others. (Self directed anger).
5. When a person is harmed or criticized by others.
6. Memories of traumatic or enraging events.

Even if anger does not result in violence, if expressed in other un-constructive ways, it can lead to broken family relationship, school suspension, lost jobs and other diminished opportunities for success that can put young people at greater risk for criminal activities.

Medical Causes Of Anger:

Personality Disorders

6. Paranoid personality disorder: Individuals with

this disorder have a pervasive distrust and suspiciousness of others and interpret their motives as malevolent.

7. Antisocial Personality Disorder - Individuals who fail to conform to social norms with respect to lawful behavior.
8. Deceitfulness, repeated lying, cornering others for personal profits or pleasure.
9. Borderline Personality Disorder - pattern of instability in interpersonal relationship, self - image, intense anger or lack of control of anger with frequent display of temper.
10. Narcissistic Personality Disorder - patient has pervasive pattern of grandiose sense of self-importance.
11. Obsessive Compulsive Personality Disorder - person has pervasive pattern or person has pre-occupation with orderliness and perfectionism interfering with task completion.

Substance abuse disorder

2. Alcohol and alcohol related disorder
3. Drug abuse e.g. Cannabis, opium, cocaine, caffeine, other hallucinogens

Paranoid psychosis

Manic episode / Hypomanic episode

There are 3 basic style of anger in people

1. The suppressor style

2. The ventor style

3. The manager or director style

The suppressor style sits on or suppresses anger. The person feels that anger is all bad and therefore must be suppressed at all cost. However anger is a natural emotion that cannot be eliminated or suppressed for long.

In the ventor style, the person freely and uncontrollably expresses their anger. These people have no mercy at the heat of moment.

The manager or director style of anger management is usually aware of his anger and uses it in constructive manner. This is probably the best way to manage anger.

- ·To deal with anger and anger provoking situations effectively and at a comfortable pace.
- ·To deal with anger that helps to resolve the situation and G To see that intervention does not increase or worsen the existing situation.

There is a difference between being assertive and aggressive. Assertive behavior is a sign of maturity and of a positive thinking person. Assertion means expressing ones rights without encroaching on other's rights and making them realize, in a peaceful manner, that you are right and the opposite person is wrong.

Anger Management

1. Rational Emotive Therapy

2. Rational Emotive Behavior Therapy

3. Psychotherapy

4. Relaxation Therapy/Progressive Relaxation Therapy.

5. Yogic Exercise

Can we make anger work for us? The answer is Yes.

Feeling angry can be beneficial if it motivates us to make necessary changes in our lives and personality. Anger should remind us that we have the power to overcome the obstacle. If we can follow the following equation then we can turn our anger to our advantage:

Anger = Energy = Power

Your anger is like a laser beam. Aim it precisely where it will do you good.

Children and adults can learn the positive values of treating each other with respect and taking responsibility for their own behavior.

Anger Management should include following steps

1. Accept that you get angry and there is a need for change in yourself.

2. Make conscious effort to change your attitude and behavior, each time you realize that a situation has provoked anger, which may require

a. Change of thoughts

b. Change of expressing words

c. Change in emotions

d. Change in external expression - behavior

3. If possible ask yourself the question “will the objective of my anger matter 10 years from now?” After getting the answer we will see things from a calmer perspective about our reactions of anger.

4. Counting from 1 to 10, either forward or backward, before reacting to any provoking situations will be helpful.

5. Consider alternative interpretation in the upsetting situation.

6. Questioning and changing our negative assumptions.

7. Changing the self-take, and the inflammatory vocabulary that triggers the use within.

8. Identifying the triggering stimuli, learning and adapting to alternative behavior, constructive avoidance and disengagement.

9. Relaxation training-especially Progressive Relaxation training, learning to monitor and reduce ones physical state of tension so that anger doesn't wear you down or lead to further aggression.

10. Associate yourself with people who have positive orientation and thinking.

11. Regular exercise to relax one self.

12.Be honest to self and to others.

13. Accept shortcomings of your life.

Suggestions

- Eliminate sarcasm and sarcastic humor from your mind and your daily attitude/behavior.
- Make humor a priority, read jokes, watch funny movies, try to incorporate laughing into your daily routine. This diffuses situation that used to make you tense and defensive.
- Develop empathy. When someone criticizes you, focus on them and their feelings, and try to imagine how they are feeling. The ability to empathize with others quickly is the hallmark of emotional maturity.

Postpone responses in conversations that provoke anger in you. Physically stop your tongue and breathe especially during heated discussions. You can buy time by saying "I will need time to think about it".

Bitter truth: Anger is dangerous to you

We've all seen these people: the boss who blows her top when a meeting runs five minutes late, the man in the coffee shop who screams and rants when his latte isn't made with soy milk, the maniac driver who honks at every car in stop-and-go traffic.

Maybe some of us actually are those people.

Aside from being annoying, and sometimes even

threatening, angry people aren't doing themselves any favors. A growing body of research suggests they may be setting themselves up for everything from heart disease and irritable bowel syndrome to headaches and maybe just the common cold.

The latest research – a study of 5,600 Italians, published this month in the journal of the American Heart Association – found that individuals who are cynical, manipulative, arrogant or short-tempered have thicker carotid arteries, which means they're more vulnerable to heart attacks and strokes.

What's doing the damage is stress and how angry people react to it – or overreact to it, mental health experts said.

"It's sort of like idling the car too high on the traffic light – you're going to be racing your engine when you don't need to," said Dr. David Spiegel, associate chairman of psychiatry and behavioral sciences at Stanford University School of Medicine. "There are times when it's right to get angry. But if your characteristic response is anger, it's really a failure to deal with stress."

'Fight' hormone

When people face a stressful situation, their bodies produce the hormone cortisol. Under normal circumstances, cortisol helps maintain blood pressure and the body's fluid balance; in a stressful situation it is what causes the heart to beat faster and sweat to break out.

The rush of cortisol is great when people face a legitimate, immediate danger. It stimulates the "fight or flight" mode that was life saving for our human ancestors. It primes the body to run fast and make quick decisions. But it is potentially damaging for people who tend to get angry and aggressive under stress, or who are chronically stressed out.

Over time, chronic stress can weaken the immune system or, alternatively, send it into overdrive, which can lead to autoimmune disorders. Chronic stress may be a cause of inflammation, which can negatively affect almost every part of the body, from the cellular level on up. Inflammation may be a cause of thickened arteries.

The Italian study focused on antagonistic traits – such as cynicism, arrogance and manipulative behavior – and how they might be related to thick carotid artery walls. It found that the people who were most antagonistic increased their risk of arterial thickening by 40 percent.

Mental health experts who read the study said that people who view the world from an antagonistic perspective – who think everyone's out to get them, and who don't trust others - are almost definitely quick to anger, and also more stressed and vulnerable to heart disease, than people who are evenly tempered.

"Basically, every dimension of the body is affected by stress. It's very clear in terms of hypertension and renal disease that stress is bad," said Dr. Laura Davies, a child and adolescent psychiatrist with California Pacific Medical Center. "There's really nothing that isn't affected by this negative outlook on life, and if you can change that, that'd be great."

Anger control

The next obvious question, doctors said, is whether people can improve their health by controlling their anger. People with extreme anger problems - those who have personality disorders or who are physically abusive - would probably benefit from one-on-one therapy. People with less immediate problems might consider anger management classes or support groups for people with hot tempers.

But many people may not know whether their anger is affecting their health, some doctors said. It may feel like their anger is a natural response to a situation, especially in the moment.

People who worry that they have an anger

problem should look at recent instances when they lost their temper, and, with the benefit of hindsight, ask themselves whether they overreacted, mental health experts say. For example, did that barista really deserve to be yelled at for flubbing a latte?

People also should pay attention to what their friends, co-workers and family members are telling them - if peers are saying that you have an anger management problem, chances are there's some truth to it, Spiegel said.

"It's like with drinking - if you've gotten drunk a couple of times in the last year, you're a human being. If you've done it every night for the past two weeks, you've got a problem," Spiegel said. "Every once in a while, many of us lose it. If it's a pattern, it's a problem."

Calming down

For most people who think they have an anger problem, the key is to get themselves calmed down in the situation. They might take a few deep breaths and give themselves time to think about what's going on, and whether it's worth getting angry about. They might need to go off by themselves for a while.

Exercise is almost always a good outlet for stress of all kinds, said Dr. Don Mordecai, director of mental health and chemical dependency services for Kaiser Permanente Northern California.

"For some people it's best to stop and take deep breaths, for some it's best to walk away, for other people it's go for a run. But in all cases, it's really that very conscious, 'Here it is, I'm angry, I recognize it, and I'm going to shift my response,' " Mordecai said. "We can spend all day thinking the world is out to screw us, and we're going to screw it back, or we can try to be good to ourselves."

Signs of a problem

- People often tell you you're overreacting.

- In past situations when you've gotten angry, the events don't seem to have justified your response.

- You get into fights - verbal or physical - regularly.

- You often feel angry when faced with stress.

Tips

What to do when stress is making you angry:

Talk to someone: People who talk calmly about what is wrong tend to feel better.

Take deep breaths: And stop to think before reacting.

Walk away: Leave a stressful situation before you get any angrier.

Get exercise: Go for a walk or a run.

Get help: Anger-management classes may help, but make sure someone with professional training runs them. Find a support group. Get one-on-one therapy.

Anger management

Here are signs that you may have an anger problem:

- People point it out to you. They often tell you to calm down or that you're overreacting.

- Looking at past situations when you've gotten angry, the events don't seem to have justified your response.

- You get into fights - verbal or physical - on a regular basis.

- You often feel angry when faced with all kinds of stress.

Here are tips on what to do when stress is making you angry:

- Talk to someone. People who talk calmly about what's wrong tend to feel better and be healthier.

- Take deep breaths and stop to think before reacting.

- Walk away. Leave the scene of a stressful situation before you get any angrier.

- Get exercise. Go for a walk or a run.

    - Get help. Anger management classes may help – but make sure someone runs them with professional training and experience. Find a support group. Get one-on-one therapy.

Honoring God with Our Capital

Honor is a heart issue. When we honor something, we allow it to influence us heavily. Likewise, when we honor *someone*, we take their advice to heart, making it the final authority in our lives. We give them the utmost respect.

God and His Word are one, and we cannot honor Him without honoring His Word. And when we honor God, He will honor us. On the other hand, in those areas where we refuse to give His Word priority, we will be lightly esteemed by Him (1 Samuel 2:30). Throughout the Bible, He tells us the ways in which we can reverence Him, which includes honoring Him with our capital (finances).

For example, Proverbs 3:9-10 in the Amplified

Bible says, *"Honor the Lord with your capital and sufficiency [from righteous labors] and with the firstfruits of all your income; So shall your storage places be filled with plenty, and your vats shall be overflowing with new wine."* In other words, one way we demonstrate our respect for God is by giving first fruit offerings (the best portion of any additional income we may receive). This scripture also tells us that honoring God with our money causes us to have financial abundance.

Here are a few other ways we can honor God with our capital:

7. We honor Him by not robbing Him of the tithe, which is a tenth of all of our income (Malachi 3:10).
8. We also honor Him by supporting His causes, which include giving financially to churches and ministries that give to the poor, spread the Gospel, and teach people how to live their lives according to God's Word.

As Believers, we cannot listen to the words of those who live by society's standards—those who may tell us that investing in the Kingdom of God is ridiculous. That is far from the truth. There is honor that only God can give us. However, we can only experience this honor when we give His Word priority in our lives. And unlike the success that comes from society, the success we receive from God has no strings attached to it.

Many times, we see others prospering in the world or society and think their prosperity is true prosperity. However, it is not. True prosperity comes from God, in the form of His blessing. The blessing of the Lord makes us rich, and there is no sorrow with it (Proverbs 10:22). Further, His provision not only frees us from the sorrows of the world, it also overflows into other areas of our lives because the blessing is an empowerment to prosper in every area of our lives. In other words, God's blessing gives us total life prosperity, which is more than acquiring money and material things.

When we honor God, we become recipients of the blessing. Therefore, I encourage you to read Proverbs 3:9-10 out loud, over and over, on a daily basis until it takes root in your heart. Then you, too, will enjoy the benefits of honoring God with your capital.

Proverbs 3:9-10

New King James Version (NKJV)

9 Honor the Lord with your possessions, And with
the first fruits of all your increase; 10 So your
barns will be filled with plenty, And your vats will
overflow with new wine.

Defining YOUR Success

If You Don't Know What You Want, You Won't Know When You've Gotten It.

When it comes to your life, do you know what you want? How does your money fit into that?

If you can't answer these two questions, you won't ever know when you've been successful In fact, it might be worse than that: you might achieve what you thought you wanted, or what all of your friends want, and then ask yourself is this it? In order to make sure you're going the right direction for you, it's important to figure out what you want from your life (to find your definition of "success" because success without fulfillment is failure).

Why It Works

We're all going after something. That's part of being alive. As long as we're living and taking action, Any action that moves you in the direction of your desired outcome is "on the right track" as progress only happens when a decision is made, just remember the definition of decision is to cut off, to sever, leaving no other option or alternative. Just remember the story of troy, find your driving force, your leverage, and be resolved in your commitment. We are all headed towards something. Even if we don't want to live, we're going towards our goal (yes, even death is a goal!). Our lives are going somewhere. We're caught up in the stream of living and we will end up somewhere so it may as well be somewhere you want to be.

Thankfully, we have some say about where we end up. We have the ability to decide what is important and make choices towards that outcome. If you're saying, "Sure, we all know that.

Make this article worth reading, already!" then tell me what you're living for. Go ahead; tell me what your life's goal is. Tell me why you're on this earth and how all the different parts of your life fit into that.

If you can do that, you're ahead of most of the population. Deciding what we want, what we're about, takes a lifetime of deliberate, focused introspection. We can figure out different parts of this whole at different times in our lives, and we can live deliberately towards them.

How it Works

If you're not sure how to get started in this process, here is a process that helps.

1. Take out a blank sheet of paper. In 10 minutes, list as many things as possible that you have not done, that you would regret not doing if you died tonight. To the best of your ability, don't stop writing and don't censor or even think too hard about anything. Just write. You might find some crazy things coming out the end of your pen, and that's OK. This isn't about being perfect or anyone else but you.

2. Read your list. Notice any internal reactions you have to different items on the list. Note these in the margins next to your list so you can remember them later.

3. Step away from the project for 24 hours no more than 2 days, except to read your list. This lets the list process in your mind. Often, writing down our desires brings to the forefront things that we haven't thought about in a while, or voices things we avoid voicing any other time.

It can take us a few days to become accustomed

to these things being a reality in our lives. We learn to accept, “Yes, I am the person whose life won’t feel complete if I never help children find their passion,” or, “definitely, I’m the busy entrepreneur who really wants a 9 to 5 job so I can spend more time with my kids before they leave home.”

4. Come back to the project and read the list again. Note any internal reactions that have changed as you let the ideas process.

5. Start pulling the different items on your list together and write a statement that encompasses what you’re about. In the beginning, this can be a list of more general categories that cover all of the items on your list.

For instance, my list would contain such items as “helping people grow” and “working with groups to help them better understand and support each other.” My larger category might be, “working with people, as individuals and in groups, to help them better understand and support the growing process in themselves and others.

Eventually, this statement will be less like a list and more like a sentence or two, but the list is fine to start.

6. Write down and commit to one step you can take this week, today, right now, to help move

your life more in alignment with your statement. Make sure that this is small enough to be achievable and is something you can maintain.

7. Repeat steps 3-6 until you have a statement that feels right. Most people know when they've hit on the one that's right for them. It moves many to tears, but some also feel joy or peace deep within when they find it. Continue with the small goals until your life looks like what you want it to be.

8. Live the life you've designed. Achieve your definition of success.

6 Simple Rituals To Reach Your Potential Every Day

Becoming and staying productive isn't about hard-to-follow programs or logging your every move in an app. It's about self-care. Here are daily to-dos to get you started.

It's Tuesday morning at 8 a.m. Two San Francisco entrepreneurs are pitching their ventures to potential investors today. They'd both agree that this is one of the most important days of their lives. This is the story of Jane and Joe...

Jane was up until 4 a.m. putting the final touches on her deck. In fact, she spent the entire weekend fixed in her apartment, preparing the presentation. This morning, she woke up late and rushed putting together her most "investor-worthy" attire. She slammed a shot of espresso, grabbed her computer, and ran out the door feeling hungry and tired. She arrived right on time but felt anxious and flustered about the events of the morning.

Joe, on the other hand, went to sleep last night at 11 p.m., as he does most nights of the week. His presentation was ready Friday afternoon, after seven revisions thanks to feedback from advisors. He spent the weekend in nature connecting with friends. This morning, he woke up at 7 a.m., had a glass of water, ran two miles, meditated for 15 minutes, and drank a smoothie. He put on the outfit he picked out the evening before, grabbed his bag, and walked out the door. He arrived 10 minutes early, feeling confident, calm, and eager to share his vision with potential investors.

Which entrepreneur would you bet on?

And, which entrepreneur most closely resembles you?

Jane and Joe are fictional characters but having been immersed in the world of startups in both New York and San Francisco, I see a lot of Janes. They work 16-hour days, seven days per week, and wonder why they aren't getting the results they're looking for. The truth is, results don't come through hours spent. Great results often come by doing less and working smarter.

This past weekend I had the opportunity to speak with my friend Mike Del Ponte, who resembles the character of Joe. Today he launches a Kickstarter campaign for his company Soma, which aims to revolutionize the water industry using sustainable design. (It's awesome. Check it out.) Surprised by how cool, calm, and collected Mike was so close to launch, I asked him what his secret is.

"Every day I need physical energy, mental clarity, and emotional balance to tackle everything that comes my way," Mike said. "Self-care is the secret to performing at the highest level."

Here are the six simple rituals he uses to perform at his highest, which you too can begin implementing right away:

1. Drink a glass of water when you wake up. Your body loses water while you sleep, so you're naturally dehydrated in the morning. A glass of water when you wake helps start your day fresh. When do you drink your first glass of water each day?

2. Define your top 3. Every morning Mike asks himself, "What are the top three most important tasks that I will complete today?" He prioritizes his day accordingly and doesn't sleep until the Top 3 are complete. What's your "Top 3" today?

3. The 50/10 Rule. Solo-task and do more faster

by working in 50/10 increments. Use a timer to work for 50 minutes on only one important task with 10 minute breaks in between. Mike spends his 10 minutes getting away from his desk, going outside, calling friends, meditating, or grabbing a glass of water. What's your most important task for the next 50 minutes?

4. Move and sweat daily. Regular movement keeps us healthy and alert. It boosts energy and mood, and relieves stress. Most mornings you'll find Mike in a Cross Fit or a yoga class. How will you sweat today?

5. Express gratitude. Gratitude fosters happiness, which is why Mike keeps a gratitude journal. Every morning, he writes out at least five things he's thankful for. In times of stress, he'll pause and reflect on 10 things he's grateful for. What are you grateful for today?

6. Reflect daily. Bring closure to your day through 10 minutes of reflection. Mike asks himself, "What went well?" and "What needs improvement?" So... what went well today? How can you do more of it?

Whether you more strongly resemble Jane or Joe, these six rituals will help you up your game, taking your performance to the next level.

I would absolutely love to know the rituals that are most valuable for you! Leave your tips in the comments below.

The Mighty Bamboo Tree

Hope… is the companion of power, and the mother of success; for who so hopes has within him the gift of miracles. *~Samuel Smiles*

In all things it is better to hope than Despair
~Goethe
You cannot hope to build a better world without improving the individuals. To that end, each of us must work for our own improvement and, at the

same time, share a general responsibility for all humanity, our particular duty being to aid those to whom we think we can be most useful. ~*Marie Curie*

This is a wonderful article on "keeping the faith" as you pursue your dreams in life.

Keep Watering Your Bamboo Tree

In the Far East, there is a tree called the Chinese bamboo tree. This remarkable tree is different from most trees in that it doesn't grow in the usual fashion. While most trees grow steadily over a period of years, the Chinese bamboo tree doesn't break through the ground for the first four years.

Then, in the fifth year, an amazing thing happens - the tree begins to grow at an astonishing rate. In fact, in a period of just five weeks, a Chinese bamboo tree can grow to a height of 90 feet. It's almost as if you can actually see the tree growing before your very eyes.

Well, I'm convinced that life often works in a similar way. You can work for weeks, months and years on your dream with no visible signs of progress and then, all of the sudden, things take off. Your business becomes profitable beyond your wildest dreams. Your marriage becomes more vibrant and passionate than you ever thought it could be. Your contribution to your church, social organization and community becomes more significant than you have ever imagined.

Yet, all of this requires one thing – faith. The growers of the Chinese bamboo tree have faith that if they keep watering and fertilizing the ground, the tree will break through. Well, you must have the same kind of faith in your bamboo tree, whether it is to run a successful business, win a Pulitzer Prize, raise well-adjusted children, or other important endeavors and business you have been nurturing.. You must have faith that if you keep making the calls, honing your craft, reading to your kids, reaching out to your client base, that you too will see rapid growth in the future.

This is the hard part for most of us. We get so excited about the idea that's firmly planted inside of us that we simply can't wait for it to blossom. Therefore, within days or weeks of the initial planting, we can become discouraged and begin to second guess ourselves or outside influence can slow or impair our dream.

Sometimes, in our doubt, we dig up our seed and plant it elsewhere, in hopes that it will quickly rise in more fertile ground. We see this very often in people who change jobs every year or so. We also see it in people who change churches, organizations and even spouses in the pursuit of greener pastures. More often than not, these people are greatly disappointed when their tree doesn't grow any faster in the new location. Other times, people will water the ground for a time but then, quickly become discouraged. They may even start to wonder if it's worth all of the effort. This is particularly true when they see their neighbors having success with other trees. They start to think, "What am I doing trying to grow a "bamboo" tree? If I had planted a lemon tree, I'd have a few lemons by now." These are the kind of people who return to their old jobs and their old ways. They walk away or abandon their bamboo dream in exchange for a more common "sure thing."

Sadly, what many people fail to realize is that pursuing your dream will be a "sure thing" if you never give up. So long as you keep watering and cultivating your dream, it will come to fruition. It may take weeks, months, years or even much of a lifetime, but eventually, the roots will take hold and your tree will grow. And when it does, it will grow in remarkable ways.

We've seen this happen so many times. Henry Ford had to water his bamboo tree through five business failures before he finally succeeded with the Ford Motor Company.

Richard Hooker had to water his bamboo tree for seven years and through 21 rejections by publishers until his humorous war novel, M*A*S*H became a runaway bestseller, spawning a movie and one of the longest-running television series of all-time.

Another great bamboo grower was the legendary jockey Eddie Arcaro. Arcaro lost his first 250 races as a jockey before going on to win 17 Triple Crown races and 554 stakes races for total purse earnings of more than $30 million.
Now after the time of hard work by many we are starting to realize the manifestation of your dreams. This is your year, your bamboo tree is sprouting. What a gorgeous sight it will be. Remember, we all have a bamboo tree inside of us just waiting to break through. Keep watering and believing and you too can be flying high before you know it because ***Gratitude makes sense of our past, brings peace for today, and creates a vision for tomorrow.***

It Really Is The Little Things

I will be adding stories through this book hoping they will be inspirational, enlightening, and a reminder of how blessed we really are. Some may bring a smile and others tears, I hope you will allow these touching stories to speak to you in a special way, I pray they touch your heart and bring new meaning and purpose to your life

~Lisa Christiansen

When I got home that night as my wife served dinner, I held her hand and said, I've got something to tell you. She sat down and ate quietly. Again I observed the intense hurt in her eyes.

Suddenly I didn't know how to open my mouth. But I had to let her know what I was thinking. I want a divorce. I raised the topic calmly. She didn't seem to be annoyed by my words, instead she asked me softly, why?

I avoided her question. This made her hurt turn to anger. She threw away the chopsticks and shouted at me, you are not a man! That night, we didn't talk to each other. She was weeping. I knew she wanted desperately to find out what had happened to our marriage. I could hardly give her a satisfactory answer; she had lost my heart to a beautiful young vibrant woman named Jane. I didn't love my wife anymore. I just pitied her!

With a deep sense of guilt, I drafted a divorce agreement that stated that she could own our house, our car, and 30% stake of my company. She glanced at it and then tore it into pieces. The woman who had spent ten years of her life with me had become a stranger. I felt so sorry for her wasted years, time invested that she will never get back. The resources and energy expended on me, I could not take back what I had said for I deeply fell in love with Jane so dearly.

Finally she cried loudly in front of me, which was what I had expected to see. To me her cry was actually a kind of release. The idea of divorce that had obsessed me for several weeks seemed to be firmer and clearer now.

The next day, I came back home very late and found her writing something at the table. I didn't have supper but went straight to sleep and fell asleep very fast because I was tired after an eventful, exciting, fun filled day with Jane. When I woke up, she was still there at the table writing. I just did not care so I turned over and was asleep again.

In the morning she presented her divorce conditions: she didn't want anything from me, but needed a month's notice before the divorce. She requested that in that one month we both

struggle to live as normal a life as possible. Her reasons were simple: our son had his exams in a month's time and she didn't want to disrupt him with our broken marriage.

This was agreeable to me. But she had something more, she asked me to recall how I had carried her into out bridal room on our wedding day. She requested that every day for the month's duration I carry her out of our bedroom to the front door ever morning. I thought she was going crazy. Just to make our last days together bearable I accepted her extremely odd request.

I told Jane about my wife's divorce conditions. Jane laughed loudly and thought it was absurd at best. No matter what tricks your pitiful wife applies, she has to face the divorce, she said scornfully.

My wife and I hadn't had any body contact since my divorce intention was explicitly expressed. So when I carried her out on the first day, we both appeared clumsy. Our son clapped behind us, daddy is holding mommy in his arms. His words brought me a sense of pain.

From the bedroom to the sitting room, then to the door, I walked over ten meters with her in my arms. She closed her eyes and said softly; don't tell our son about the divorce. I nodded, feeling somewhat upset. I put her down outside the door.

She went to wait for the bus to work. I drove alone to the office.

On the second day, both of us acted much more easily. She leaned on my chest. I could smell the fragrance of her blouse. I realized that I hadn't looked at this woman carefully for a long time. I realized she was not young any more. There were fine wrinkles on her face, her hair was graying! Our marriage had taken its toll on her. For a minute I wondered what I had done to her.

On the fourth day, when I lifted her up, I felt a sense of intimacy returning. This was the woman who had given over ten years of her life to me. On the fifth and sixth day, I realized that our sense of intimacy was growing again. I didn't tell Jane about this. It became easier to carry her as the month slipped by. Perhaps the everyday workout made me stronger.

She was choosing what to wear one morning. She tried on quite a few dresses but could not find a suitable one. Then she sighed, all my dresses have grown bigger. I suddenly realized that she had grown so thin, that was the reason why I could carry her more easily.

Suddenly it hit me... she had buried so much pain and bitterness in her heart. Subconsciously I reached out and touched her head.

Our son came in at the moment and said, Dad, its time to carry mom out. To him, seeing his father carrying his mother out had become an essential part of his life. My wife gestured to our son to come closer and hugged him tightly. I turned my face away because I was afraid I might change my mind at this last minute. I then held her in my arms, walking from the bedroom, through the sitting room, to the hallway. Her hand surrounded my neck softly and naturally. I held her body tightly; it was just like our wedding day.

But her much lighter weight made me sad. On the last day, when I held her in my arms I could hardly move a step. Our son had gone to school. I held her tightly and said “I hadn’t noticed that our life lacked intimacy.” I drove to office.... jumped out of the car swiftly without locking the door. I was afraid any delay would make me change my mind...I walked upstairs. Jane opened the door and I said to her, Sorry, Jane, I do not want the divorce anymore.

She looked at me, astonished, and then touched my forehead. Do you have a fever? She said. I moved her hand off my head. Sorry, Jane, I said, I won’t divorce my wife. My marriage life was boring probably because she and I didn’t value the details of our lives, not because we didn’t love each other anymore.

Now I realize that since I carried her into my home on our wedding day I am supposed to hold her until death do us part. Jane seemed to suddenly wake up. She gave me a loud slap and then slammed the door and burst into tears. I walked downstairs and drove away. At the floral shop on the way, I ordered a bouquet of flowers for my wife. The salesgirl asked me what to write on the card. I smiled and wrote; I'll carry you out every morning until death do us apart.

That evening I arrived home, flowers in my hands, a smile on my face, I run up stairs, only to find my wife in the bed -dead. My wife had been fighting CANCER for months and I was so busy with Jane to ever-even notice. She knew that she would die soon and she wanted to save me from whatever negative reaction from our son, in case we push through with the divorce. At least, in the eyes of our son I'm a loving husband....

The small details of your lives are what really matter in a relationship. It is not the mansion, the car, property; it's not the money in the bank. These create an environment conducive for happiness but cannot give happiness in themselves.

So find time to be your spouse's friend and do those little things for each other that build intimacy. Do have a real and happy marriage!

Time Is The Only True Coin

Imagine there is a bank account that credits your account every morning with $86,400. It carries over no balance from day to day. Every evening, the bank deletes whatever part of the balance you failed to use during the day. What would you do? Draw out every cent of course. Each of us has such a bank. Its name is time. Every morning, it credits you with 86,400 seconds. Every night it writes off as loss, whatever of this you have failed to invest to a good purpose. It carries over no balance. It allows no overdraft. Each day, it opens a new account for you. Each night, it burns the remains of the day. If you fail to use the day's deposits, the loss is yours. There is no drawing against "tomorrow." You must live in the present on today's deposits. Invest it so as to get it from the utmost health, happiness and success.

Time is the only coin of your life and only you can determine how it will be spent, be careful not to let anyone spend it for you. Choose your own priorities. We often drift through days that are full of things we "have to do" or "should do" or what others "want us to do." Why? There are plenty of people out there more than willing to put in their two cents about your time. Every day, you'll hear sales pitches about the endless options you have and other people's opinion of what should be important to you. Have they got their own lives in such perfect order that it qualifies them to make decisions for yours? Like any purchase, it's valuable to listen, but keep that coin in your pocket till YOU decide where it will be spent. Try to see the difference between a real obligation and an imagined one. The only things you have to do are the obligations you choose. You might find that more is optional than you really think.

The clock is running...make the most of today!

The best way to become success is to study success and emulate success. Procrastination is the abortion of success. The most successful in life are the ones brave enough to step out into the unknown. ~Lisa Christiansen

Six signs of emotional blockage

EMOTIONAL RELEASE

Are you guilty of falling short of a true spring clean? The tendency this time of year is to focus on physical clutter, but the kind you can't see - emotional clutter - is just as important to tackle.

By emotional clutter we mean all those repressed, suppressed and unexpressed emotions and old beliefs that are keeping you stuck, rooted in a spot that probably no longer represents who you are or what you are capable of.

Emotional clutter acts like an invisible set of horse blinders that keep you from seeing beyond what is right in front of you. They blind you to potential paths forward and from the resources and options you have at your disposal. But because those emotional blinders aren't physical, they are easy enough to suppress or ignore.

Here are six signs you have emotional clutter to deal with, and ideas for clearing it out.

9. **Your Expectations of How Others Should Behave Is Distancing You From Them.** Do you have rules for how the people in your life need to show you they love you? For example, do you "need" your husband to start taking out recycling without being nagged to feel more appreciated? The problem with this is twofold: (a) it is extremely rare that these expectations are ever verbalized so the other person has no idea he is fouling up, and (b) your focus on what they aren't doing right often causes you to miss other, real expressions of love.
10. **What You Should Do Is Making You Miserable or Rebellious.** Just as "should" isn't a good motivator for others (see point No. 1), it's not a good motivator for you, either. Rather than bowing to "should dos," the next time you start to do something because you have to, stop. Take five minutes to consider what you really want to do and why. Then decide to make and follow your own rules in that area going forward.
11. **You Cringe Every Time You Scroll Through Your Contacts and See That Name.** Old relationships that ended on an unfortunate note, whether personal or professional, are part of life. If you had one, do yourself a favor and get some closure. Distance is the only thing that will lessen the emotional sting. Delete the contact information from your phone. UnFriend, UnLink, and UnFollow. You don't need to know

what they are up to if all it does is make you re-experience a past hurt.

12. **You Feel Guilty Because You Let Someone Down.** Human beings are born to please. From the time we can walk, we are socialized to share, pitch in and contribute. The principle of reciprocity serves as a crucial glue for our community-based societies. But it can also lead you to over-commit. If you're chronically over-extending yourself, and letting people down in the process, you need to swap your "Sure, no problem" for "That sounds really interesting; let me think about it and get back to you with an answer." Then use the time to determine whether you want to accept the request.
13. **You Get a Nagging Feeling When You Think About (Or See Contact Information For) Someone.** Sometimes so much time has passed since you last connected with someone that you feel guilty just thinking about them or seeing their information in your phone. Rather than suppressing the negative emotion, call them. Ideally, right when you realize you're feeling guilty. If you can't do it right then, make an appointment to connect with them before the week is out.
14. **You Have Uncompleted Projects.** When you fail to complete a project, you not only have physical reminders of it, but nagging emotional ones as well. The nagging may not be urgent, but it's there, somewhere in the back of your mind, constantly reminding you that you have something left to do. If you've got one (or more) of these, take some time before the day

is out to make a list of the projects you want to complete. Then break them down into smaller work steps and schedule them in. If you have a half-started project that you no longer really want to finish, it's OK. Better to let it go and be at peace with your decision than to continue to carry it around.

Emotional Blockage Release Techniques

Emotional blockages are obstacles that are preventing you from doing what you want in life. They manifest through low self-esteem, depression, anger and fear. These blockages are a result of the past, and will put a limit on your development no matter how talented or skilled you are. There are many special techniques that you can use to remove these emotional blockages so that you can move forward in life.

Affirmations

12. A good way to remove blockage is having some positive affirmations that you say to yourself on a daily basis. Repeating these affirmations to yourself will tell your subconscious to believe them. Affirmations should read something like "I feel content with myself" or "I am confident and proud of myself." Do not include what you will not do. For example "I will not be afraid anymore," this will only remind you of your obstacle.

Keeping a Journal

4. Writing in a journal or diary daily allows you to express yourself without being inhibited, which helps release emotions. You can let off some steam at someone or something that made you angry or upset during the day or you can talk about your fears. In your journal, you can also talk about your goals and plans for the future to encourage yourself to meet those goals.

Breathing Techniques

- You can use breathing techniques to take your mind off of your negative emotions. These techniques involve inhaling slowly and deeply and holding your breath for a few seconds. You will continue doing this four times. This will make you feel relaxed and refreshed. Breathing techniques help reduce anxiety.

Emotional Freedom Technique (EFT)

- An alternative technique used to release emotional blockage is called EFT, or Emotional Freedom Technique. This involves tapping on your acupressure points at the top of your head, eyebrows, the side of the eye and chin. You can also tap your wrists, collarbone and under arm. You will do this about 5 to 7 times as you acknowledge an emotional positive statement about yourself. For example, you might state, "I deeply and completely accept myself." This practice helps diminish negative emotions associated with the memory and helps remove the emotional block, according to Joseph Mercola, M.D. There are plenty of EFT practitioners who will walk you through this

process.

All of us, at one time or another have dealt with some form of emotional blockage. Most emotional blocks are the result of some type of crisis in our life whether self inflicted, environmental or cultural.

When we feel unable to deal with a crisis, we are besieged by feelings of fear, anger, confusion, anxiety, guilt, or inadequacy. We lose our ability to think rationally about our problem and find a logical solution.

One way to begin working on blockages is to do some deep breathing. We don't breathe the way we should; we generally take very shallow breaths. Breathe deeply, filling your lungs to the very bottom, and then release.

If you spend a few minutes doing this, it will calm you down, make you feel better (perhaps a little dizzy the first time you do this action step, this is normal), help stop your mental chatter and begin bringing emotional blocks to the surface for you to deal with.

Our external environment is a reflection of our internal environment. Look at your home, is it neat? Sloppy? Chances are you have a lot of clutter. Our homes are filled with so many things that we really don't need or even want. In the same way, our minds are filled with emotional clutter. There are so many bad and depressing thoughts that, for whatever reason, we have not let go of.

Understand, I don't mean that you should dwell on past crises or traumas! Quite the opposite, you should acknowledge them, forgive the situations and/or people involved, and release the block. This will free up your energy, giving you more of your power for your daily life and your Laws of Attraction that God has abundantly blessed you with will bring positive seeds to bear living fruit.

If you dwell on the bad things in your past, guess what? You're just attracting them again into your future. This is why clearing out blockages is so important. Get rid of anything negative and depressing. Fill your mind with new, refreshing, interesting and happy thoughts.

Those who have had happy pasts are far more likely to have happy futures. If you are not happy, you are likely clinging to events in the past that made you unhappy. This may not even be a conscious process. In fact, it's almost surely not conscious or in any way intentional. However, in order to bring happiness into your present and keep happiness in your future, it is important to let go of the past.

It's up to you to remove your emotional blockages. When you remove these blocks, you create a vacuum in your life that has the ability to suck in quickly whatever you are currently attracting. If you combine blockage release with Law of Attraction exercises, you will release a lot of negative feelings from your life while sucking your desires into manifestation.

If a stone in the road is blocking your path, you will both carry it and put it aside or you will roll it aside. If neither of these options is feasible, you will find a way around the stone. Likewise, some emotional blockages can be removed directly, while others need to be removed by finding away around them.

Deep breathing exercises are an excellent way to rid yourself of unwanted emotional blocks without having to be terribly active in the memory.

However you go about it, do work to free yourself of emotional garbage. Any drudgework in the short run will pay incredible dividends in the long run.

When You Thought I Wasn't Looking

A message for every adult to read; children are watching you and doing as you do, not as you say.

When you thought I wasn't looking, I saw you hang my first painting on the refrigerator door and I immediately wanted to paint another one.

When you thought I wasn't looking, I saw you feed a stray cat, and I learned that it was good to be kind to animals.

When you thought I wasn't looking, I saw you make my favorite cake for me and I learned that the little things are the special things in life.

When you thought I wasn't looking, I heard you say a prayer, and I knew there is a God I could always talk to and I learned to trust in God.

When you thought I wasn't looking, I saw you make a meal and take it to a friend who was sick, and I learned that we all have to help take care of each other.

When you thought I wasn't looking, I saw you give of your time and our only food because we had no money to help people who had wronged us and I learned that everyone has something to give and should help others no matter what.

When you thought I wasn't looking, I saw you take care of our house and everyone in it and I learned we have to take care of what we are given!

When you thought I wasn't looking, I saw how you handled your responsibilities even through your challenges, even when you didn't feel good and I learned in that moment how to be responsible.

When you thought I wasn't looking, I saw tears come from your eyes and I learned that sometimes things hurt and it's ok to cry.

When you thought I wasn't looking, I saw that you cared even when your words said you didn't and I wanted to be everything that I could be.

When you thought I wasn't looking, I learned most of life's lessons that I need to know to be a good and productive person when I grow up.

When you thought I wasn't looking, I looked at you and wanted to say, "Thanks for all the things I saw when you thought I wasn't looking."

LITTLE EYES SEE A LOT. Each of us (parent, grandparent, aunt, uncle, teacher or friend) influences the life of a child. How will you touch the life of someone today?

Peace and Love To You All ~ You reign over the unspoken word - Once you speak and release it - it reigns over you - choose wisely -

"He who is wise will keep an open mind until he has fairly tested the various proofs that are available to him"

To be persuasive, one must be believable;

To be believable, one must be credible;

To be credible, one must be truthful.

Discover Power Through Your Weakness

The Power to Never Feel Powerless Again

In one way or another, we often feel “trapped” by life. If it weren’t true, we wouldn’t spend as much time as we do trying to “escape” our circumstances. Embrace fear as your councilor and weakness as your power.

We’re so involved with imagining and swimming to

our own Fantasy Island, we never consider this important question: what if the condition we wish to escape were only an illusion that feels real? How would such a realization change our lives?

Let's look into these questions, starting with the feeling of being trapped. What do we know about it? For one thing, it is neither gender nor economically selective; everyone, regardless of socio-economic status, has a share of this unwanted state of self.

We also know that none of us would remain feeling trapped if we had the power to change our condition. Which leads us to this finding: We frequently feel powerless.

And when we see no solution to our situation, confusion colors our considerations. Frustration grows. We feel imprisoned behind a wall of fearful expectations.

We need not, and must not, accept a life of such limitation. We can uncover the root of this powerless feeling and release ourselves from it by discovering the nature of the illusion that creates it. We must do three things, first we must be honest with the situation, second we must see things better than they are not worse than they are and then we must take action to make it they way we see it.

For most of us the show gets started like this: "Why did he have to do that?" or "Life isn't fair!" or "They took this away from me." But these reasons are not the source of our pressing stress!

First we must see that these moments are events, not powers; they are passing conditions, not prisons. Seeing this, the real question isn't how to regain our lost power; the real question is "what is it about these events that causes us to feel powerless because of them?"

Here are a few vital facts: the feeling of being powerless has nothing to do with what someone else did or didn't do or with what you did or didn't do at any point in your life regardless of your present conditions. A little detective work will prove these statements. People will remain in their current state until the pleasure outweighs the pain. All human's behaviors revolve around the urge to gain pleasure or avoid pain. To get leverage is to associate massive pain to not changing now and to associate massive pleasure after you have changed it. The key is to get a lot of reasons, better, strong enough reasons to make your change now. Every long lasting change is made in your subconscious mind.

What's the first thing we see when we hear news that runs counter to what we want? We don't really "see" anything at all; instead our attention is seized, absorbed by a familiar negative reaction whose only wish is that the unwanted moment just go away.

This resistance acts on our consciousness as a "blinding" and binding force, so all we can "see" is our own negativity over what we wish wasn't happening! We literally "look" at what we don't want to be there and what you focus on is what you get.

For example, when expectations get dashed, we don't see new possibilities unfolding; all we see is the way things should have gone. We don't see what is with all of its positive possibilities; instead we see only the negative . . . what is not.

We feel powerless because we've become the captive of a mind resisting itself, an involuntary prisoner of a mind struggling to escape its own negative images. There is nothing but powerlessness in this resistance because by law whatever we resist… persists!

The only way to liberate ourselves from the confines of this unconscious relationship is to develop a new awareness of what it costs us to remain in its captivity.

We must ask, what kind of "power" is it to resent any moment for unfolding as it does, to wish it didn't happen? Does it change the moment in any positive way? No, it does not.

Does our pain prove that our position is right? To the contrary: the more we don't want the moment, the more we lend credibility to that moment as being overpowering. This false perception then strengthens our negative sense of self as someone who is being overpowered by it.

But this next insight foretells freedom: whenever we feel like a powerless captive of some condition, it's because we grabbed onto a false power to lend us strength. Worry, fear, anger, self-loathing, self-pity. . . all negative states are a waste that consume our lives whenever we embrace their empty promise of empowerment.

By contrast, real power is in knowing we already possess everything we need to succeed in any moment. Let's examine this important idea.

What good is any conditional power, social or financial if when a challenging moment comes along, we can't count on that power to be there for us?

We've all seen what happens when due to "unscheduled changes" our power source is suddenly unplugged.

We either collapse into powerlessness, or scramble around searching for ways to regain our base of power. Either way, we remain a captive of these reactions.

People become angry when they realize they don't possess the power they imagined. They justify this imagined loss by blaming others for it, and now their power is in being resentful.

Real power keeps us from becoming the puppet of what is unkind to others and ourselves. Real power lifts us above challenging circumstances; it shelters us from fears that want to drag us down into troubled thoughts about tomorrow. Real power is the quiet and certain understanding that everything that comes to us works for the good of us, no matter what it is.

How do we enter into relationship with such pure power? We begin with a startling insight:

Human beings have mistaken themselves as being powers unto themselves. The truth is, we are the instruments of elemental powers, high and low; recognize our unique place in reality gives us a far greater role to play than any of these primal forces can ever hope to know.

We alone are empowered to choose from all powers, potential or present which of them we will embody and serve by expression.

Although we often find ourselves feeling so there is no such thing as being powerless. Those who resist life who hate or fear unwanted changes become the instrument of a power that effectively renders them powerless to do anything but struggle.

But those who realize that the only power negative states have is to create the illusion of self-command, enter into relationship with another kind of power altogether. And this new awareness, like the power it grants, is failsafe.

We can practice this true, new power anytime we want its strength and safety. We start by remembering that in any moment of heartache, worry, or fear, we need not suffer what comes with resisting our sense of being powerless because ours is the power to choose what we will and will not give our power to. The following examples reveal this new and higher possibility:

Rather than live with the pain of a thousand regrets, we can realize that no number of visits to a painful past can change it. The light of this new awareness empowers us to start over now.

Rather than look to anxious thoughts to help us through some fearful situation, we can see that anxiety serves fear, so how can it free us from it? The light of this new awareness empowers us to let go of both these impostors.

Rather than defend our mistakes by excusing them, we can understand that our refusal to learn the lesson at hand ensures we will meet that lesson again, along with its misery. The light of this new awareness empowers us to accept what life would teach us, and the truth sets us free.

Negative states want to convince us we are powerless in the face of what frustrates us. Once we see that this false perception is actually produced by a dark state that would have us turn to it for the power we need to make things right.

We are learning we can do something radically new: rather than give ourselves over to the habitual reaction of resisting the moment for our fear of it, we remember the truth that sets us free: ours is the power to live from the Power of our choice.

Said slightly differently: we are created with the power to surrender our sense of powerlessness and, in exchange for this sacrifice, realize a life without stress and strife.

Whenever we have a pain or a problem that seems greater than we can deal with, it doesn't mean we really are without power. These moments are actually "wake-up calls" invitations to remember our relationship with an indwelling Divine order of ourselves that is the same as our True Nature.

This new action on our part, this conscious realignment born of higher self-awareness, is the same as our rescue. Our sense of being powerless is replaced by releasing the misunderstanding over who we really are.

Now the words, “Let go and let God” take on new meaning. We now understand what must be done to let the Divine Light do for us what we can’t: to know true power, we must release all claims upon it.

Those With Whom We Assemble, We Resemble

Free Yourself From Toxic People (You Are Your 5 Closest Friends)

Don't let
negative & toxic people
rent space in your head.
Raise the rent &
kick them out.

Those with whom we assemble, we soon resemble!

This simple old saying hides a deep Truth that can enlighten and empower every aspect of our lives:

Who we are, our very essence, is continually being transformed by the company we keep.

Better said, when we keep the company of what is positive, happy, healthy, wealthy and wise, our lives become more positive, happy, healthy, wealthy and wise. When we keep the company of what is negative, disempowering and discouraging, our lives can't help spiraling downward from it's current state.

This idea might sound a little simplistic at first, but its power soon becomes evident when we put it to use in the quest to realize our highest aspirations. The key lies in understanding that this principle is active on multiple levels at once.

For instance, when referring to "the company we keep," we of course mean the people we spend time with every day such as family, friends, co-workers, etc.

However, **on a deeper and more important level, "company" can also refer to the thoughts and feelings moving within us in any given moment.**

Have you ever been home alone in a fine mood, enjoying a meal perhaps, only to find yourself bored or depressed an hour later? That's a perfect example of the effect of hanging out with the wrong interior friends.

When we are unconscious to the operation of our minds, any indigent thought or feeling that passes through us has the power to strike up a conversation and drag us into its dark circle of influence.

Just as it is possible for us to keep bad interior company that pulls us down, so is it possible to keep positive inner company that works to raise us up in any moment we choose to remember it.

This means that **we can choose not to get dragged down when we are alone**, it also means that **we can choose not to get dragged down when we find ourselves in the presence of negative people as well.**

How encouraging! When life places us in a situation where a run-in with someone is inevitable, perhaps at work, with a family member, in a store, etc. **We can choose to keep the company of good and true interior friends who can help keep us from falling into negative states**.

And therein lies the key: when we remember that keeping the company of negative interior friends is a choice, instead of an obligation, we are free to keep the company of compassion instead of anger, generosity instead of greed, and patience instead anxiety.

Building on this idea, let's look at four common types of people that can be identified by the four prevailing dark states that inhabit them. By learning to recognize and understand the interior workings of these four types of "toxic people," we gain important insight into what is dark and limiting inside of us.

In this way, we begin the process of liberation from everything inside of us that stands in the way of knowing the peace, happiness, success, and love that we long for.

1 Past Progressives: These negative spirits live to drag up old painful events and then revel in the anger, resentment, or bitterness that such unhappy memories hold. Stay away from any spirit, in others or in yourself, that wants you to dive into some suffering over what happened in any past event.

2 Emotional Vampires: These malicious spirits pull themselves up by pulling others down. They love to gossip, criticize, judge, and denigrate anyone who ever had the misfortune of spending time with them. The only loyalty these denizens of the unconscious worlds have is to their own pain, which they feed by involving everyone they can in their mud slinging.

3 Subconscious Succubus: There is a group of mired spirits that thrive on low vibrations, and that require a human instrument to play out their endless dark dissonance. Easily recognizable, these misfortunate forces serve up dreadful mental pictures of past and future events for the sake of the unnatural reactions they produce. Ignore these corrupted spirits and they must take their evil speculations elsewhere.

<u>4 Living Dead:</u> These dark spirits perpetuate their hold on the human soul by resisting the beautiful gifts of life. They trick us into commiserating with their complaining, cruelty, and irritation because without our unconscious consent, these chronically conflicted spirits can't spread their poison.

Just as harmful viruses require a human host to exist and thrive, so do negative states require the unconscious consent of human beings to carry out their dark mission. For what power does a negative thought have other than the power to convince a person to do its bidding? The answer is none!

When we begin to consciously withdraw our consent to associate with toxic people, toxic thoughts and feelings inside of us, we leave them with no place to thrive. Our real inner work is to sweep clean the places in ourselves where such creatures reside which in turn brightens our life and the lives of everyone around us.

Begin today, this very moment, to withdraw any permission you have unknowingly granted these dark spirits to be in your life. Do not judge yourself, or those around you in whom these misdirected forces are active, instead come awake and refuse to spend one more moment of your life lending your precious life force to their dark purposes.

This powerful, positive action will change your life. As you begin to refuse to consort with what is dark, you'll find that you begin to attract with what is light, bright, and cheerful. Your relationships will deepen, your professional life will take on new vigor and freshness, and the whole of your days will begin to resemble the radiant Life that you have deliberately chosen as your conscious companion.

The 20 Essential Habits of Highly Passionate People

WHEN THE WHY's BECOME CLEAR → THE HOW's BECOME EASY

I've always worked hard at whatever I've been doing. My work ethic comes from doing what I enjoy, and not forcing myself to do something.

Highly passionate people aren't just lucky they share common characteristics. They work hard, they trust their intuition and they persevere.

I personally don't see myself having any other options than following my passion. Without doing what I truly want, life would be without color, without joy and without meaning. Success without fulfillment is failure.

We all have the habits necessary; we just need to let them shine.

1. Excitement

When I was in my late teens, I wasn't even remotely familiar with terms like "follow your passion", "listen to your heart" or "go with your intuition".

As the years have passed, these concepts have grown and I've realized that the only thing that matters is what I am excited about in this very moment.

It's far too easy for me to start questioning what I'm doing. Let's take language learning for example. It's easy for me to argue that it's a waste of time.

But in the end, what matters is how much I'm enjoying myself. You can never know where you'll end up, so you might as well enjoy the ride, right?

We've been taught that logic is superior, but is it really? Life isn't a game where all the variables are known, so there's no way you can predict the future (unless you have special powers).

2. Courage

Courage is something you build up. When I was younger, I was afraid a lot more than I am now, but I didn't let it control my life.

Many seem to believe that following their passion should be effortless. Fortunately it's not, because if it were everyone would be doing it like a cookie cutter mold. It requires a lot of hard work, but the good news is that you'll love it because you're doing something you're excited about.

I've never worked a real job in my life. I have always owned my own business from the moment I turned 2 years old and all through my life, even when there wasn't a profit I always believed it would come. I had no idea I was going to succeed at the level I am at now and I still see myself as the little girl from Tahlequah, Oklahoma. In the beginning, a lot of people doubted if making a living speaking was possible.

I have a passion for helping others, so I keep at it and eventually I started making a comfortable living. That took courage, but it wasn't extraordinary. I just took things one day at a time and worked hard.

3. Determination

If there's anything I've learned, it's that results usually don't come fast. Following your passion doesn't just happen. It takes a lot of hard work. In my case, I invested a lot of money before I started making money.

People tell me that I'm lucky. I seem to get good at everything they say. I'm not lucky. I'm

just determined and I make sure to pick something that I like doing. It's pretty easy to get good at something you love doing.

In the beginning, you may not be 100% determined, but that's okay. Be as determined as you can be and keep moving forward. Many people mistake a temporary failure for a permanent one.

There are no permanent failures. There are only learning opportunities. If you learn everything you can about blogging, try it for a year and then lose motivation—that's cool!

You never know. Maybe you unconsciously picked up a few skills that will help you down the road with something else.

My #1 priority is doing what I feel excited about.

4. Positivity

I have bad days like anyone else, but in general I'm a pretty positive girl. I feel good as long as I'm doing what I feel I should be doing.

There's a fine line between being blissfully ignorant and positively realistic. It's something you have to figure out for yourself. Try both and find your own balance.

I personally enjoy being blissfully ignorant, especially if it upsets someone else. There are a lot of people out there that try to tell you that you can't go after your dreams.

Those are dream thieves and they are usually the people that have given up. They aren't really in a place to give advice. Giving their comments energy is allowing them to live rent free in your head.

By being positive you lead by example. There is really no better way to change the world than to be the change you want to see. There's no need to convince anyone.

5. Single-Mindedness

Being passionate doesn't mean limiting yourself to one passion per lifetime. I've been passionate about health, martial arts, websites and languages.

My passion changes all the time, but what remains constant is my single-mindedness. I work best when I'm 100% focused on what I do.

For example, in 2010 I immersed myself in mastering NLP. I did nothing else but study NLP for several months. I'm obsessive like that.

I want to be able to spend as many hours as

possible on what I truly enjoy. That is what I mean by being single-minded.

6. Growth-Oriented

By following your passion, you automatically become growth oriented. You tap into something greater than yourself.

That source of guidance can only lead to one place and I think you know what it is. We all have different words, definition and concepts about it, but we all mean the same thing.

I'm always looking to grow in every way possible. I want to become better, smarter and happier.

You must keep it fun.

Let's say you have to choose between two paths.

Path #1 is faster, but requires more discipline and is less fun. Path #2 is slower, but you'll enjoy it more. In the past I would've chosen Path #1, but now I'd choose #2, because if I'm not enjoying myself right now, it's not worth it.

7. Selective

I used to have a problem of jumping into too many things at once. I think we all have many

interests, which is good, it can be a double-edged sword.

I think we're familiar with the feeling of wanting to do everything at once. Usually when I ask someone what they want to do, they rabble up a dozen different things.

What works for me is relentless focus. I pick one thing, maybe two, and focus on them until I feel like it's time to move on.

For some, this may seem irresponsible, but to me, it's the only way of living life that makes sense.

8. Non-Perfectionistic

Imperfection is perfection, I'm a Virgo and apparently they are perfectionists. I am no exception so I must remind myself that imperfection is perfection.

Throughout the years I've learned to ease up on my perfectionism. Instead of focusing on the little details, I've started focusing on the big picture.

I think about what I want to achieve and I am more concerned about making progress than making everything look good.

Let's take blogging as an example, just because

it's on my mind right now. If you want to start blogging, just start! You don't need an awesome design or to have everything planned out.

All you need is to get your blog up, get it looking okay and start writing, recording podcasts or making videos. That's the only way you'll know if you even like it.

So often we think we like something, but when we actually start, we realize that it doesn't feel right at all. That's why it's important to get started, get your feet wet and see how it feels.

9. Prioritized

Prioritization goes hand in hand with being selective. I know people that don't have time, and I know people that make time. It's not that you don't have enough time; it's that you fail to prioritize.

I've received a lot of e-mails about time issues. I know some people are single-mothers, working two jobs while juggling two kids. I know how tough that is, I also know that if you really want something, there are ways to make time and prioritize, even if it starts with a few minutes per day.

No matter how tough your situation is, you can always do something to move towards your

goals. Don't worry about reaching your goal just worry about making today more fulfilling than yesterday.

10. Self-Motivated

As long as I'm doing what I want to be doing, I don't need self-motivation. It's only when I do the boring tasks that I have to throw in some Wonder Woman motivation techniques.

For example, when I was working on Living Your Passion, I had to get the technical part fixed in order to start selling it. It wasn't fun, but I knew that it had to be done.

My focus was constantly on how good I would feel when I was done. Whatever motivates you is fair game. There are no rules when it comes to self-motivation.

I sometimes use negativity to motivate myself. I don't care, as long as I get things done. I try to be proactive and avoid these situations though.

The more I follow my passion, the more motivated I am.

11. Acceptance

Sometimes things don't work out the way I want them to. I do my best to accept whatever comes my way, but I don't always succeed. Sometimes life just isn't that easy.

If there's something I focus on impressing to portray, it's the fact that I'm as human as you. Even seemingly "perfect" personal development experts are human.

We all make mistakes. We're all afraid. The people that seem to be the most successful are the ones who've figured out how to keep taking action despite the obstacles on their path.

There's no one out there that can really tell you what to do. You have to figure out your own stuff. While I do recommend that you learn from others in the beginning, you also have to be willing to take the wheel after awhile and start experimenting.

12. Generous

Service to others is really service to self. I'm going to say that one of the main reasons I want to help you is because it makes me feel good to see you succeed.

I've been on both sides of the fence. When I was a professional exercise and nutrition master trainer, I was focused largely on myself.

It was nice, it just wasn't fulfilling. I've since discovered that helping others makes me feel much better than just helping myself.

Something I also want to point out is that sometimes you need to help yourself before you can help others. Looking at it from that perspective, personal development is really world development.

13. Non-Balance

I have a tendency to get obsessed about the things I am interested in. Like I mentioned above with my NLP training. When I started this blog back in 2009, I was obsessed. I read, listened and did nothing but consulting. It was all I wanted to do.

And it helped me go from 0 to 2,000 fans on facebook in 90 days without ads. When you take action, results happen.

The most important thing is that I had fun while doing it.

I work best when I'm non-balanced. I may do something 10 hours a day for 3 months and then take a break, or I may do it less. It all depends on how I'm feeling.

14. Personal Power

When I got out of school at 18, my personal power level was very low. As the years passed,

I've realized that the best place to look for guidance is within. If you've been reading my wordpress, you know I say that a lot.

This has helped me build confidence. I by no means have a perfect guidance system. I fall into traps. I make a fool of myself, and that's okay, because I know that I would not want to be doing anything else.

We all have a kid inside of us who wants someone to tell us what to do. We want validation and all that good stuff. That's okay, just remember in the end, you are the only one who really knows what you want.

15. Happiness

I used to think money was the answer to happiness. The only way to happiness was having millions in the bank and relaxing on a nice white beach, that no longer interests me because I know the artificial happiness it creates would not last.

I need something to work on. I am constantly being pulled in different directions, and I love it. If I were to take a "vacation", I'd probably get bored after a week and start looking for something to do.

We don't really need to retire to a beach in

Italy. All we need to do is find what makes us tick, to find our passion(s).

I couldn't imagine myself doing nothing for an extended period of time. Happiness to me is doing what I want. It may mean something different for you, but that's what it means for me.

16. Fun

There's a need for discipline and there's also a need for fun. I used to be a lot more disciplined than fun. I'd say no to requests to hang out, because I had my eyes on my current goal.

I wanted to reach my goal as soon as possible. I wanted to get things done. I'm not going to say that I've overcome this, because I love my obsessions too much, I've gotten a lot better at relaxing and having fun.

There's no rush. If you feel like taking a break, then take a break. Who cares if you reach your goal? Who cares how good you look on paper? Who cares what other people think?

17. Perspective

It's easy to get bogged down in the details, which is why it's important to take a few steps back and look at what you're really trying to achieve.

I have a very easy time falling into the trap of looking at numbers on my social media pages. I look at how many people subscribe to my e-mail list and the thank you e-mails I receive.

I am guilty of comparing myself to others and think about how far I still have to go instead of looking at how far I've come.

In the end what this all comes down to is following my excitement. I have to remind myself of that once in awhile. I have to remind myself that I can relax and enjoy myself.

I have to remind myself that there's no rush. The only pressure you experience is the pressure you put on yourself.

18. Dream The Impossible

When you dream the impossible the incredible happens. Most of the things we today take for granted were thought to be impossible in the past. The simple point I want to make is this: don't listen to the "Nay Sayers," because you will run into plenty of them.

I enjoy being called UNREALISTIC because that's when miracles show up. If I feel good about something, I'll go for it. I don't care if the chances of me succeeding are small, because even if it doesn't work out, I will most likely gain some vital experience points in life.

If at some point you don't doubt yourself, you're probably not being uncomfortable enough. Going after your passion means being uncomfortable. It's not necessarily a bad thing it's just different.

19. Open-Minded

Being flexible and open-minded means different things to different people. I like to think of myself as open-minded.

If I've set my sails for something, I shut out everything else and start taking action. There's no need for me to keep distracting myself with more information if I know enough to take action.

There will always be people telling me that I'm doing things wrong, I don't listen to them, because the only thing that matters is how I feel about what I'm doing.

Maybe I need to fail in something to succeed at something else down the road. This is why I've stopped looking at things in isolation. I've started to trust the force.

20. Excuse-Free

Last, but definitely not least is the fact that I don't take excuses seriously. If I want something badly enough I will overcome any excuse.

If I succumb to my excuses, I know I'm not really ready to head down that road. It may also be because it's not a road that's a good fit for me at this time.

When I'm on-fire about something, excuses fly out the window. When I started studying NLP, I knew that I could make a living if I put in the work.

I was afraid, shy and had all the usual problems 18-year olds have, but my goal was to make it work. I didn't want a 9-to-5 job like everyone else. It just wasn't for me.

The excuses you have right now don't matter. What really matters is what kind of life you want.

From Worrier to Warrior

Knowledge is not the same as wisdom, wisdom is doing. Everyone wants to tell you what to do and what's good for you, they don't want you to find your own answers because they want you to believe theirs. Stop gathering information from outside of yourself and start gathering it from the inside, people are afraid of what's inside and that's the only place you are ever going to find what you need. Why can't you sleep? is it because late at night when you're alone and the silence screams you get a little scared because everything feels so empty? do you feel like you are losing your mind? sometimes you have to lose your mind to come to your senses. Maybe it's because you want to be someone who uses his mind and his body in ways that most would never have the courage to, maybe it's because you are destined to be a real warrior to serve others instead of being a worrier of self-loathing. To be a warrior is to be shielded in Gods armor of his perfect design with his word as your sword, the holy ghost as your army, and his love as your joy that brings you authentic peace. A warrior is not about perfection or victory, or invulnerability, a warrior is about absolute vulnerability. That's the only true courage.

The mind is just a reflex organ, it reacts to everything. It is the mind you must conquer because where the mind goes the body will follow and once you master your emotions you are in control of your destiny. It's all about leverage, life is about developing the wisdom to apply the right leverage in the right place at the right time. Take a personal inventory of your life and "take out the trash" everything that is negative and not serving you is "trash." The trash is everything that is keeping you from the only thing that matters, this moment, here, now. When you are in the here and now you will be amazed at what you can do and how well you can do it. Are you in the past gloating, holding on to attachments, are you in the past vengeful letting your emotions control you, are you living in reaction or are you in the present living on purpose? all you have is right now.

A warrior acts only a fool reacts, death isn't sad what is sad is that most people never live fully and a life lived in fear is a life half lived. Stop holding on to the past because all you have is right now and if you knew you had one minute to live and were to ask yourself "have I really lived" could you say "YES, passionately, fully, and I am so exhausted I am ready" because I want you to experience everything you love and love everything you experience, find the beauty where there was none. Remember, when you don't get what you want you suffer and when you get what you want you still suffer because you can't hold onto it forever. Pride of oneself and genuine love for others cannot coexist therefore one must give up what one cannot keep to get what one cannot lose... Understand that just because things don't always work the way you want you don't give up on your dreams you give up the only thing you never had, control, realize that either way whatever happens you are exceptional.

Be "present" and live fully engaged in the moment to experience life fully with the knowledge that there is never nothing going on, there are no ordinary moments, make time to experience the timeless moments of the lives around you because you may be the only person who is a witness to another's existence and the beauty of their life. The people that are the hardest to love are usually the ones who need it the most, you will never be better nor will you ever be less, just be conscious of your choices and responsible for your actions. Every action has it's price and it's pleasure, recognizing both sides and is becoming realistic and responsible for your actions.

Life has three rules, paradox, humor and change, life is a mystery don't waste time trying to figure it out, keep your sense of humor especially about yourself because it is a strength beyond all measure, know that nothing stays the same.

The journey is what brings us happiness not the destination; ask yourself these three questions,

1. Where are you? here
2. What time is it? now
3. What are you? this moment...

10 Reasons for A 10 Week Gratitude Journey

10 Reasons for A 10 Week Gratitude Journey

Reach more goals: Participants who kept gratitude lists are more likely to make progress toward important personal goals (academic, interpersonal, and health-based even weight loss) than those who did not.

Improved Health: The study also showed physical changes; the authors reported those keeping gratitude journals exercised more regularly and reported fewer physical and emotional symptoms.

Better Sleep=More Energy: The Study included a group of adults with neuromuscular disease who underwent a “gratitude intervention” for three weeks. Afterward, participants reported improvements in both how much and how well they slept.

Stronger Love Life: According to the study, feelings of indebtedness showed engagement and commitment externally yet gratitude had uniquely predictive power in relationship promotion, perhaps acting as a booster shot for the relationship.

Support Others: Participants in the daily gratitude condition were more likely to report having helped someone with a personal problem or having offered emotional support to another, relative to the hassles or social comparison condition.

Increase Influence: Gratitude generates social capital, in two studies with 243 total participants, those who were 10% more grateful than average had 17.5% more social capital and that number compounded by the level of increased gratitude.

Gratitude can lower your blood pressure: Robert Emmons, professor of psychology at the University of California, Davis and "the world's leading scientific expert on gratitude" says that people who keep gratitude journals "show a 10 percent drop in blood pressure compared to persons who are not keeping these journals."

Gratitude Boosts our Mental Health: Researchers affirm that gratitude can also boost our mental health and well-being. They found that people who kept notes on what they're thankful for have reported higher levels of positive emotions, **more joy and pleasure, more happiness and optimism.** They felt **more alert, alive, and awake** than others who did not practice gratitude. Notably, people who are focused on things they are thankful for are less depressed and less angry. In fact, researchers have found that **gratitude can increase your "set point of happiness" by 25 percent.**

Practicing gratitude can also enhance our relationships with other people. For example:

Gratitude can ward off envy: Robert Emmons points out, "You cannot feel envious and grateful at the same time. They're incompatible feelings. If you're grateful, you can't resent someone for having something that you don't." His research has suggested that people who have high levels of gratitude have low levels of resentment and envy.

Gratitude can even help you attain your goals.

Participants in a study who were asked to keep gratitude lists were more likely than those in control groups "to have made progress toward important personal goals (academic, interpersonal, and health-based) over a two-month period."

A Simple Way to Tap Into Gratitude's Benefits

How do you tap into some of these great benefits? It's simple. At the end of the day, take a moment to write down what you're grateful or thankful for. Write one phrase or sentence per each gratitude, up to five. That's it! Participants in studies who have done this have reported significant benefits after just two weeks.

Join the 10-Week Gratitude Challenge

Are you willing to accept a little challenge? Let's join together in keeping gratitude lists once a day for 10 weeks, and let's see if we experience any of the benefits I've listed above. If we make our first gratitude lists today and then continue for 9 more weeks, we will complete the 10th entry on Tuesday August 6, 2013.

Let's plan to touch base at that point and see if we are healthier and happier.

My Gratitude Journal

Write a word or draw a picture on the blank line.

I AM grateful for__________.

I AM grateful for__________.

I AM grateful for__________.

I AM grateful for__________.

I AM grateful for__________.

I AM grateful for__________.

I AM grateful for__________.

Girls Compete With Each Other, Women Empower One Another

I hope you will read this with an open mind and a gentle receiving heart, the same as it is from the one posting it. May it enlighten you to more about life, other women, and yourself. May it encourage you to make changes that will make you feel better about yourself and may it inspire you to be that mentor to younger women struggling to make their way in this troubled world.

There comes a time in every woman's life when she has to take a close look at herself. Not at her circumstance, not at what she did, not how unfair life is or not at who made you do it. She has to just look at herself in all her glory and imperfection.

For many women, this is a scary thing because often times they don't want to know the truth about themselves. Virtuous women know what I mean.

As women, we have a tendency to water one another down. Maybe it makes us feel good or look better than the next woman. Or maybe we just don't know how to tell that woman how we admire her.

In reality, we really WANT to look at ourselves and the pain we project towards other women.

Have you ever admired a woman who has been through changes in her life? Or have you made up in your mind that she is just messed up.

Before you make this mistake, take a close look.

The women who have endured the most abuse, mistreatment and/or pain in life are the chosen by God filled of wisdom. Someone who has been chosen by God to go through so that others may be enlightened is a role model for the afflicted.

Think of all the great women in the bible, Mary Magdalene, Ruth and Naomi, The woman with an issue of blood, and Esther, to name a few. Mary

was a very uneasy woman.

By the time God was done with her, she was His closest follower. Esther was unfortunate in marrying an abusive man.

By the time God was done with her, she married one of the wealthiest men in the land.

Have you ever admired the strength of a single mother? Or have you made up your mind that it's too bad she had children on her own.

A single mother knows no bounds when it comes to her children. She is strong and durable. Single mothers are strong, not because she has to be, but because it comes naturally for her to protect the extensions of her very being.

Her love for her children is like that of fuel to a car. Most mothers keep their tanks full because they understand that, if it runs low, you could jeopardize the car and have problems in the long run.

Other women only fill it when it is needed. Their cars usually break down.

Have you ever wondered why some women are not approachable? Or have you made up your mind that she is just mean.

A quiet woman is a smart woman. She is valuable.

She doesn't go off half-cocked and she won't be the one to argue with you over nothing. She just may even let you go on "setting her straight" and politely back out without a fight. She doesn't let many in her world.

After all, she has probably been through the fire and had to rebuild. So why let just anyone in? This is usually the woman that only has "small talk" and knows her place, which is away from all the unnecessary things in life.

Have you ever wondered why that woman is so loud? Well, hey she has a lot to say. These are usually our younger women who have to learn refrain.

They are eager and unsettled. They talk before they think, and they do not think before they talk. They just go.

Have you ever wondered about that woman who appears to have everything, yet is still very unhappy? Well, she doesn't have everything. She doesn't have personal validation.

This is something that cannot be bought. This is something developed over many mistakes and challenges that have taught lessons of the unbearable.

Women are so quick to beat the next one down

instead of trying to hold her up. Before you wonder, "What's up with her?" ask yourself, "What's up with me?" Why do I beat down another woman to build myself up?

That woman could be my mother, sister, aunt, in-law, stepmother, niece, grandmother, great-grandmother, neighbor, friend, co-worker, etc. That woman could just be me.

Women are the carrier of life, not the channel of death. Let's build and encourage each other, as did Ruth and Naomi.

Encourage and Love, Forgive and Forget, trust that the woman that receives this will be touched in some way.

Peace and Love To You All

~You reign over the unspoken word, once you speak and release it, the unspoken word reigns over you so choose wisely.

"He who is wise will keep an open mind until he has fairly tested the various proofs that are available to him"

To be persuasive, one must be believable;

To be believable, one must be credible;

To be credible, one must be truthful.

My passion for life has always been fueled through serving the needs of others by helping others achieve their dreams. I have found that by helping others I receive paychecks of the heart that money cannot replace, the joy I see on a mothers face when she no longer struggles to feed her family is truly priceless. The relief I see in a woman's eyes who no longer has that tired look of not knowing how her day was going to end because her future was in the hands of her abuser is what I thrive on because I too was once her. The excitement I hear in a woman's voice because she has a successful business earning a six-figure income when she remembers a time when she did not know how she was going to pay the rent is simply a blessing. The respect I see in husbands' eyes for his wife who has grown from a timid girl into a strong, independent, and successful woman is a sight to behold. I have been all of these women. I want this for all of you!

As you come to know me better my hope is that you will feel the pride that I have lived with in my Cherokee heritage. I am active in the Cherokee nation, the Chamber of Commerce, and the Rotary. I specialize in teaching others to become Independent, not co-dependent. I wish to think that my specialty is not as a teacher but as an example.

I choose to live by example and follow a great leader rather than lead by ignorance.

Live Like Today Is Your Last

Find your peace because life is short, if asked when will you die the answer is so simple that it's complicated... "in one breath" Life ends with a breath and death begins with a breath... live like today like it is your last because somebody took your place today, make them proud...

~Lisa Christiansen

Beyond The Limits of Possible Lives The Impossible

The only way to discover the limits of the possible is to go beyond them into the impossible...

- Choose mastery

- Study the subject of the experts of your desired outcome and interview other experts, intensely looking for patterns and best practices.

• Create arguments on what to pay attention to and what things mean; how things might turn out and focus on the solution..

• Simplify complex ideas by building frameworks.

• Write, Speak, record and package their knowledge backed by your expertise.

• Campaign (not promote) their expertise and bring your expertise to the table for the ultimate result.

History is on no ones side what matters most is what we do...

Ask God To Open Your Eyes

Ask God to OPEN YOUR EYES to see what is already in you.

(Ephesians 1:18, Ephesians 3:20).

The Holy Spirit is in you. The Love of God is in you. Faith is in you. These forces of God's power are in you right now. Affirm this, I am complete in Christ. There is no good thing missing in my life. I have all things in Him. My God supplies all my needs, and I expect His supply TODAY. I have the peace of God, which delivers my heart from trouble and disappointment. Even if people let me down, my God will uphold me and help me. I have the Holy Spirit, the love of God and the gift of faith in my life. I am complete in Him, in Jesus' Name! Amen

~Lisa Christiansen

In One Breath

Find your peace because life is short, if asked when will you die the answer is so simple that it's complicated... "in one breath" Life ends with a breath and death begins with a breath... live like today like it is your last because somebody took your place today, make them proud...
~Lisa Christiansen

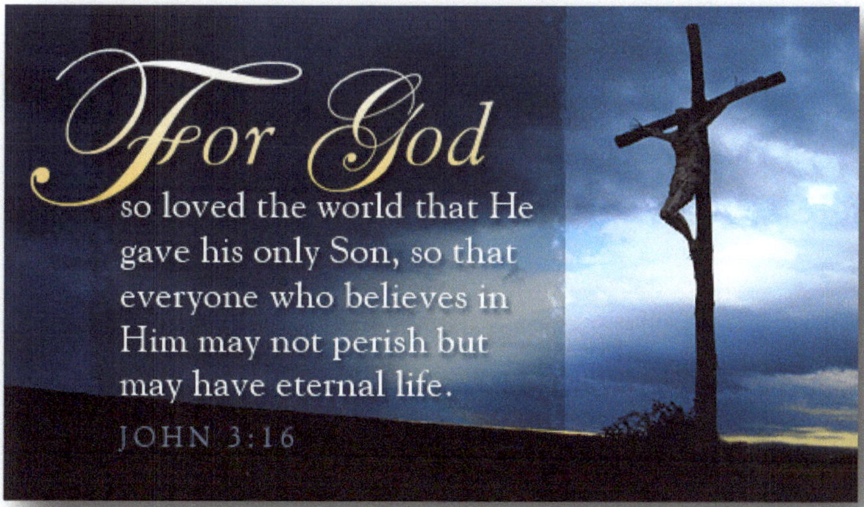

I Come To You In Humble Gratitude

I believe that we must go where we are needed as did Christ not making ourselves exclusive to the righteous, we must embrace non-believers and believers equally with the word of God as we share the everlasting love of Jesus Christ through the gift of the Holy Ghost as we are commanded by God to keep our eyes upon him. I appreciate your prayers and will return the favor by praying for our Holy Father to soften our hearts and open our soul to submit to God's will completely. I pray for our spirit to be freed from the chains of bondage so our childlike innocence may once again shine bright and allow each of us to breakthrough to the freedom of loving all of God's Children equally. I pray for each of you a life filled with a happiness born from the womb of joy, love born from Gods design, and health born from the healing hands of Christ's blood shed to flow through our veins offering gratitude embraced in the Holy Spirit. I pray this in gratitude for the blessings that I am so abundantly gifted with, I am grateful for the blessings placed before me today and everyday as I continue to find strength in faith through the power of the Holy Ghost, the love of Christ while embraced in Gods infinite grace. I pray for the lost to find their way and for God's mercy to rest upon those that have passed without accepting Christ for their salvation that they may be spared and given a home in heaven even if it means my soul must take their place... Amen

Love Is You...

When you feel it say it because moments will pass, life will fade, it is only love you take with you when God calls upon you and say's "tonight your soul is required of thee" Love is the only thing we get to take with us when this life is over, love is what endures, love is what lives and love is what conquers all else... Love is the essence of us and it is my love for each of you that I will carry forevermore into the heights of heaven as our love will soar and dwell in the heavens for all to observe in awesome wonder as I do everyday in God's grace...

Love Is What We Are Born With, Fear Is What We Learn

Welcome fear as your councilor, fear is here to serve you not to imprison you in your own self-paralysis...

Life is constantly testing us for our level of commitment and life's greatest rewards are reserved for those who demonstrate a never-ending commitment to act until they achieve. It is this level of resolve can move mountains only if it is constant and consistent. As simple as this sounds, it is the common denominator separating those who live their dreams from those who live in regret.

To Receive One Must Give

Proverbs 11:24-25

24 Give freely and become more wealthy; be stingy and lose everything. 25 The generous will prosper; those who refresh others will themselves be refreshed.

ᎾᎯᏳᏃ ᎯᎠ ᏄᎵᏍᏔᏁᎢ, ᎾᏍᎩ ᏏᏌ ᎣᎦᏍᏓ ᎤᏁᏨᎯ ᎤᎾᏄᎪᏤ ᏂᎬᎾᏛ ᎡᎶᎯ ᎨᎦᏎᏍᏗᏱ. ᎾᏍᎩ ᎯᎠ ᎤᎾᏎᎵᏙᎴ ᎠᏏ ᏌᎵᏂ ᏏᏓᏱ ᎤᎬᏫᏳᎯ ᏂᎨᏒᎾ ᏥᎨᏎᎢ. ᎠᎴ ᏂᎦᏛ ᎤᏁᏅᏎ ᎨᎦᏎᏍᏗᏱ ᎠᏂᏏᏴᏫᎭ ᎨᏒ ᏙᏓᏂᏚᎲᎢ. ᎠᎴ ᏦᏩ ᎾᏍᏉ ᎨᎵᎵ ᎤᏂᎩᏎᎢ ᎤᏄᎪᏤ ᎠᏎᎵᏗ ᎦᏋᎲᎢ, ᏭᎷᏤ ᏧᏗᏱ, ᏕᏫ ᏧᏪᏚᎲᎢ, ᎦᏚᏱ ᏧᏙᎢᏛ, ᏕᏫᏰᏃ ᎤᏁᏢᏔᏅᏛ ᎨᏒ ᏅᏓᏳᏓᎴᏅᎯ ᎨᏎᎢ ᎤᎦᏴᎵᎨ ᎨᏎᎢ ᎠᎴ ᏕᏫ, ᎨᎦᏎᏍᏗᏱ ᎤᏰᎸᏎ ᎤᏰᎸᏎ ᎤᏩᏒ ᎠᎴ ᎺᎵ ᎤᏓᏴᏍᏗ, ᎾᏍᎩ ᎦᏁᎵᏛ ᎨᏎᎢ. ᎯᎠᏃ ᏄᎵᏍᏔᏁᎢ, ᎾᏍᎩ ᎠᏏ ᎾᎿ ᎠᏁᏙᎲᎢ, ᎤᏍᏆᎸᎲ ᎠᏲᎵ ᎤᎾᏄᎪᏫᏍᏗᏱ. ᎤᎾᏄᎪᏫᏎᏃ ᎢᎬᏱ ᏂᎯ ᎤᏪᏥ ᎠᏧᏣ, ᎠᎴ ᎤᏪᏣᏄᏔᏁᎢ, ᎠᎴ ᏐᏈᎵ ᎤᎾᎵᏍᏓᏴᏗᏱ ᎤᎸᏁᎢ; ᎥᏝᏰᏃ ᏳᏜᏅᏕ ᏧᏂᏒᏍᏗᏱ ᎠᏓᏁᎸᎢ. ᎾᎿᏃ ᎾᎥᎢ ᎠᏫ-ᏗᏂᎦᏘᏯ ᎠᏁᏙᎲ ᎤᏜᏅᏛᎢ, ᎠᏫ ᏓᏂᎦᏘᏰ ᎡᏃᏱ. ᎬᏂᏳᏉᏃ ᏗᎧᎿᏩᏗᏙᎯ ᏱᎰᏩ ᎤᏤᎵᎦ ᎤᏂᎷᏤᎴᎢ, ᎠᎴ ᎦᎸᏉᏗᏳ ᏚᎸᏌᏛ ᎤᎬᏫᏳᎯ ᎤᏤᎵᎦᏚᏫᏚᏫᏍᏔᏁᎢ ᎠᎴ ᎤᏣᏔᏅᎯ ᎤᏂᏍᎦᎴᎢ. ᏗᎧᎿᏩᏗᏙᎯᏃ ᎯᎠ ᏂᏚᏪᏎᎴᎢ; ᏝᏍᏗ ᏱᏥᏍᎦᎢᎮᏍᏗ, ᎬᏂᏳᏉᏰᏃ ᎢᏨᏲᎯᏏ ᎣᏍᏛ ᎧᏃᎮᏛ ᎤᏣᏘ ᎠᎵᎮᎵᏍᏗ, ᎾᏂᎥ ᏴᏫ ᎤᎾᏛᎪᏗ. ᎪᎯᏰᏃ ᎢᎦ ᎢᏣᏕᏁᎸ ᏕᏫ ᎤᏪᏚᎲᎢ, ᎢᏥᏍᏕᎵᏍᎩ ᎾᏍᎩ ᎦᎶᏁᏛ

ᎤᎬᏫᏳᎯ. ᎯᎠᏃ ᎾᏍᎩ ᎢᎶᏙᎯᎱᎯᏍᏙ ᎨᏎᏍᏗ; Ꮭ ᏱᏥᏩᏛᎯ ᎠᏲᎵ ᎠᏥᎶᏄᎴᏍᏗ, ᏐᏈᎵ ᎤᎾᎵᏍᏓᏴᏗᏱ ᎦᏅᎨᏍᏗ. ᎩᎳᏉᏃ ᎢᏴᏛ ᎤᏂᏣᏘ ᎦᎸᎳᏗ ᎠᏁᎯ ᎬᏩᎵᎪᏁᎴ ᏗᎧᎿᏩᏗᏙᎯ, ᎤᏁᎳᏅᎯ ᎠᏂᎸᏉᏗᏍᎨᎢ, ᎯᎠ ᎾᏂᏪᏍᎨᎢ;

"ᎦᎸᏉᏗᏳ ᎨᏎᏍᏗ ᎤᏁᎳᏅᎯ ᏩᏍᏛ ᎦᎸᎳᏗᏳ, ᎡᎶᎯᏃ ᏙᎯᏱ ᎨᏎᏍᏗ, ᎣᏍᏛ ᎨᎦᏓᏅᏖᏍᎨᏍᏗ ᏴᏫ."

ᎿᏉᏃ ᎯᎠ ᏄᎵᏍᏔᏁᎢ, ᎾᏍᎩ ᏗᏂᎧᎿᏩᏗᏙᎯ ᎬᏩᎾᏓᏅᏒᎸ, ᎦᎸᎳᏗ ᏫᎤᏂᏣᏒ, ᎯᎠ ᏂᏚᎾᏓᏪᏎᎴ ᎠᏫ-ᏗᏂᎦᏘᏯ; Ꮼ, ᎿᏉ ᎦᏚᎲ ᎢᏕᎾ, ᎠᎴ ᏫᏓᏙᎴᎰᎯ ᎾᏍᎩ ᎯᎠ ᏄᎵᏍᏔᏅᎢ, ᎾᏍᎩ ᏱᎰᏩ ᎬᏂᎨᏒ ᏥᏂᎬᏂᏏ. ᎤᎵᏍᏗᏳᏃ ᏭᏂᎷᏤᎢ, ᎠᎴ ᏚᏂᏩᏛᎮ ᎺᎵ ᎠᎴ ᏦᏩ, ᎠᎴ ᎠᏲᎵ ᏐᏈᎵ ᎤᎾᎵᏍᏓᏴᏗᏱ ᎦᏅᎨᎢ. ᎤᏂᎪᎲᏃ ᎤᏂᏃᎮᎵᏙᎴ ᏄᏍᏛ ᎨᏥᏃᎮᎮᎸ ᎾᏍᎩ ᎠᏲᎵ ᎠᏥᏁᎢᏍᏗᏍᎬᎢ. ᏂᎦᏛᏃ ᎤᎾᏛᎦᏅᎯ ᎤᏂᏍᏆᏂᎪᏎ ᏄᏍᏛ ᎬᏩᏂᏃ ᎮᎮᎸ ᎠᏫ-ᏗᏂᎦᏘᏯ. ᎺᎵᏍᎩᏂ ᎾᏍᎩ ᎯᎠ ᏂᎦᏛ ᎤᏍᏆᏂᎪᏔᏁᎢ, ᎠᎴ ᎾᏍᎩ ᎤᏓᏅᏖᎯᎶᏒ ᎴᏓᏅᏛᎢ. ᎠᏫᏃ-ᏗᏂᎦᏖᏯ ᎢᎤᎾᏨᏎᎢ, ᎠᏂᎸᏉᏗᏍᎨ ᎠᎴ ᎠᎾᎵᎮᎵᏤᎮ ᎤᏁᎳᏅᎯ ᏅᏗᎦᎵᏍᏙᏟᏍᎨ ᏂᎦᎥ ᎤᎾᏛᎦᏅ ᎠᎴ ᎤᏂᎪᎲᎢ, ᎾᏍᎩ ᏄᏍᏛ ᎨᏥᏃᏁᎸᎢ.

Luke 2:1-20 The Birth of Jesus

2 In those days Caesar Augustus issued a decree that a census should be taken of the entire Roman world. 2 (This was the first census that took place while[a] Quirinius was governor of Syria.) 3 And everyone went to their own town to register.

4 So Joseph also went up from the town of
Nazareth in Galilee to Judea, to Bethlehem the
town of David, because he belonged to the house
and line of David. 5 He went there to register
with Mary, who was pledged to be married to him
and was expecting a child. 6 While they were
there, the time came for the baby to be born, 7
and she gave birth to her firstborn, a son. She
wrapped him in cloths and placed him in a
manger, because there was no guest room
available for them.

8 And there were shepherds living out in the fields
nearby, keeping watch over their flocks at night.
9 An angel of the Lord appeared to them, and the
glory of the Lord shone around them, and they
were terrified. 10 But the angel said to them, "Do
not be afraid. I bring you good news that will
cause great joy for all the people. 11 Today in the
town of David a Savior has been born to you; he is
the Messiah, the Lord. 12 This will be a sign to
you: You will find a baby wrapped in cloths and
lying in a manger."

13 Suddenly a great company of the heavenly host
appeared with the angel, praising God and saying,

14 "Glory to God in the highest heaven, and on
earth peace to those on whom his favor rests." 15
When the angels had left them and gone into
heaven, the shepherds said to one another, "Let's
go to Bethlehem and see this thing that has

happened, which the Lord has told us about."

16 So they hurried off and found Mary and Joseph,
and the baby, who was lying in the manger. 17
When they had seen him, they spread the word
concerning what had been told them about this
child, 18 and all who heard it were amazed at
what the shepherds said to them. 19 But Mary
treasured up all these things and pondered them
in her heart. 20 The shepherds returned,
glorifying and praising God for all the things they
had heard and seen, which were just as they had
been told.

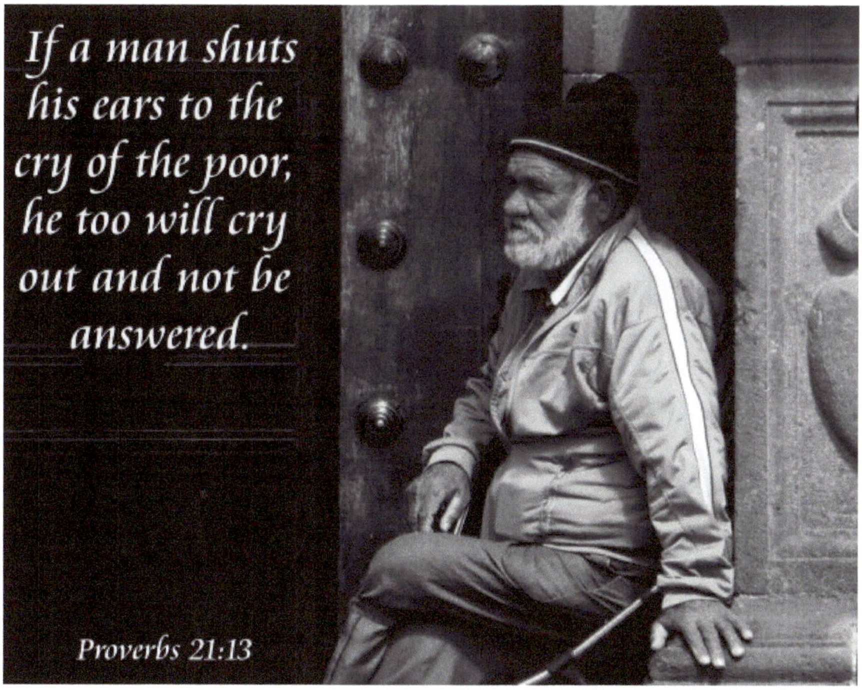
If a man shuts his ears to the cry of the poor, he too will cry out and not be answered.
Proverbs 21:13

Gratitude + Forgiveness = Grace

Duress impacts relationships in one of two ways, it either tears people apart or strengthens their connection binding them tightly in a common objective. The most intense conflicts, if overcome, leave behind a sense of security and calm that is not easily disturbed. It is just these intense conflicts and their conflagration which are needed to produce valuable and lasting results.

Even a happy life cannot be without a measure of darkness, and the word happy would lose its meaning if it were not balanced by sadness. It is far better take things as they come along with patience and equanimity. Every one of us, unconsciously, works out a personal philosophy of life, by which we are guided, inspired, and corrected, as time goes on. It is this philosophy by which we measure out our days, and by which we advertise to all about us the man, or woman, that we are. . . . It takes but a brief time to scent the life philosophy of anyone. It is defined in the conversation, in the look of the eye, and in the general mien of the person. It has no hiding place. It's like the perfume of the flower unseen, but known almost instantly. It is the possession of the successful, and the happy. And it can be greatly embellished by the absorption of ideas and experiences of the useful of this earth.

The most important human endeavor is the striving for morality in our actions. Our inner balance and even our very existence depend on it. Only morality in our actions can give beauty and dignity to our lives. Always question where your loyalties lay, the people you trust will expect it. Your greatest enemies will desire it and those you treasure the most will without fail abuse it. Loyalty inspires boundless hope, and while that may be there is a catch, true loyalty takes years to build and only seconds to destroy.

Genuine forgiveness heals any hurts or wrongs. It strengthens the disheartened soul that has lost its way. It refreshes and renews our hope. It is through forgiveness that we are "born again" and "become like a child." In this way we regain the precious attitude of a willing mind that is ready to learn all over again. Know that your most precious, valued possessions and your greatest powers are invisible and intangible. No one can

take them. You and you alone, can give them. By giving you will receive abundance for your giving. You will receive paychecks of the heart that money cannot replace.

Woman Of Worth

Woman the very matrix that God sent salvation to the world through, God puts the definition of woman of church to be his bride so God highly esteems woman, alter your perception of woman to Gods and build yourself as woman upon this foundation and dwell in his glory as it is an honor to be called woman. Do not let anyone change the definition of "woman" by their ill treatment or their words for you are a true blessing and the chosen one to bring forth life into this world and for some it is to nurture life that would not exist without you.

A woman strengthens her man through nurturing affection with appreciation.

Religion is man searching for God and Christianity is God searching for man

It has been said that a sinner is someone who knows God and a priest is someone in search of God. Religion is man searching for God and Christianity is God searching for man.

The Love Letter

Recently I posted about writing a simple note just to say “thank you” to someone for making a difference in your life even if you don’t know the person because the act of writing a person you don’t know can change your life by the gift of making a difference in their life... You may be the only person who ever made them feel love, life or maybe just that they mattered enough to someone to think of them. Thank you to everyone for loving me and celebrating the lives of others with me... The best way to find yourself is to lose yourself in the service of others, what I mean by this is pride of oneself and genuine love for others cannot coexist therefore one must give up what one cannot keep to get what one cannot lose...

20 Actions For 20 Days

Below you will find 20 actions, apply 1 a day for 20 days until all 20 actions become a part of who you are. Today is the first day of the rest of your life, I challenge you to begin a small group of accountability to bring abundance into your life of positive results (professionally and personally) because when you make a conscious decision to write at least one "thank you" note to friends, clients and sometimes even new acquaintances every day for a year you will begin to live in gratitude naturally.

1. Rise with the sun to pray. Pray alone. Pray often. God will listen, if you only speak.

2. Be tolerant of those who are lost on their path. Ignorance, conceit, anger, jealousy and greed stem from a lost soul. Pray that they will find guidance.

3. Search for yourself, by yourself. Do not allow others to make your path for you. It is your road, and yours alone. Others may walk it with you, but no one can walk it for you.

4. Treat the guests in your home with much consideration. Serve them the best food, give them the best bed and treat them with respect and honor.

5. Do not take what is not yours whether from a person, a community, the wilderness or from a culture. It was not earned nor given. It is not yours.

6. Respect all things that are placed upon this earth – whether it be people or plant.

7. Honor other people's thoughts, wishes and words. Never interrupt another or mock or rudely mimic them. Allow each person the right to personal expression.

8. Never speak of others in a bad way. The negative energy that you put out into the universe will multiply when it returns to you.

9. All persons make mistakes. And all mistakes can be forgiven.

10. Bad thoughts cause illness of the mind, body and spirit. Practice optimism.

11. Nature is not FOR us, it is a PART of us. They are part of your worldly family.

12. Children are the seeds of our future. Plant love in their hearts and water them with wisdom and life's lessons. When they are grown, give them space to grow.

13. Avoid hurting the hearts of others. The poison of your pain will return to you.

14. Be truthful at all times. Honesty is the test of ones will within this universe.

15. Keep yourself balanced. Your Mental self, Spiritual self, Emotional self, and Physical self - all need to be strong, pure and healthy. Work out the body to strengthen the mind. Grow rich in spirit to cure emotional ails.

16. Make conscious decisions as to who you will be and how you will respond. Be responsible for your own actions.

17. Respect the privacy and personal space of others. Do not touch the personal property of others, especially sacred and religious objects. This is forbidden.

18. Be true to yourself first. You cannot nurture and help others if you cannot nurture and help yourself first.

19. Respect others religious beliefs. Do not force your belief on others.

20. Share your good fortune with others. Participate in charity.

Sounds easy enough until you start to actually do it, and then all the excuses come out. Like many things in life I am not going to say it's going to be easy, I am saying it will be worth it, so my quick note to you is:

• Thank you for your support, guidance and most of all your friendship... it is appreciated! Thank you.

• Gratitude is the mother of all emotions, I choose to live in forgiveness and gratitude because forgiveness will set you free to live in gratitude and until you do this you will live in bondage. When you decide to live in forgiveness that is when gratitude thrives and only then will success show up beyond your expectations. Remember, forgiveness is a valuable gift that is neither easily obtained, nor easily given. Forgiveness is essential for life, forgiving others offers the gift that frees us of our past wrongs and and enables us to love with a renewed strength for the one we once felt wronged us.

forgiveness will set you free...

Dreams pass into the reality of action. From the actions stems the dream again; and this interdependence produces the highest form of living. Most people can look back over the years and identify a time and place at which their lives changed significantly. Whether by accident or design, these are the moments when, because of a readiness within us and a collaboration with events occurring around us, we are forced to seriously reappraise ourselves and the conditions under which we live and to make certain choices that will affect the rest of our lives. Gratitude is the key to success, forgiveness is the key to gratitude... forgiveness will set you free...

Splendid Sinners

This is a much-needed word for a generation of Christians with an inflated sense of self-importance. Apart from God's grace, even our best efforts are nothing more than "splendid sins." In my better moments, which are all too few, I realize that even my best efforts fall well over into the "splendid sins" category. Ryle has told the truth about the best of us and the rest of us. This side of heaven, we're a pretty sorry lot, but that's where God's grace comes in. No one will be saved by what they do. Our only hope of heaven is to run to the cross and lay hold of Jesus Christ. And we won't even do that unless God helps us to do it, and even then he must give us the strength to hang on and to keep believing.

Apart from God's grace, even our best efforts are nothing more than "splendid sins." We are all ...

Splendid sinners, Lovable losers, Miserable misfits, and Fantastic failures.

Consider the roll call of God's imperfect heroes:

The talent pool has always been pretty thin when it comes to moral perfection. Noah who got drunk. Abraham who lied about his wife. Jacob who was a deceiver. Moses who murdered an Egyptian. Rahab who was a harlot. Samson who

had serious problems with lust and anger. David who was an adulterer. Paul who persecuted the church. Peter who denied Christ.

If God chose only well-rounded people with no character flaws, some of the credit would inevitably go to the people and not to the Lord. By choosing flawed people with a bad past, a shaky present, and an uncertain future, God alone gets the glory when they accomplish amazing things by his power.

In case we don't understand this, 1 Corinthians 1:26-31 makes it abundantly clear. If you want the message of this passage in one sentence, here it is: God won't tolerate human pride, so he chooses people who have nothing to brag about.

The Reason Given

"But God chose the foolish things of the world to shame the wise; God chose the weak things of the world to shame the strong. He chose the lowly things of this world and the despised things—and the things that are not—to nullify the things that are, so that no one may boast before him" (I Corinthians 1:27-29). In these verses Paul makes his teaching even clearer. God chooses "weak things" and "lowly things" and "despised things" and even "things that are not." These "things" are actually people—weak people, lowly people, despised people, and people who are invisible to

the world. In short, God makes a choice, and the choice he makes is to choose the people the world would never choose. The words of Isaiah 55:8 come to mind, "'For my thoughts are not your thoughts, neither are your ways my ways,' declares the Lord." Here's a simple way to remember this truth: God is different. Ponder that statement for a moment. God is different from us. He is different in what he thinks and he is different in what he does. He does not do what we expect him to do because his thinking is entirely different from ours. He nullifies the mighty by using the weak instead. He nullifies the proud by using the humble. He nullifies the wise by using the simple. He nullifies the professional by using the blue-collar worker. He nullifies the PhD by using the high school dropout. God's "nullification" demonstrates how fundamentally different he is from us. This truth—elementary as it may seem—is actually quite vital to a healthy Christian worldview. Our God stands alone. He does not bind himself to do what we think he ought to do. He is holy and he is sovereign and he is absolutely free to do whatever he pleases to do. He can humble the proud any time he chooses. No one has the power to stand against him.

God does it this way for three reasons:

1) To destroy all human pride, 2) So that no one can boast, and 3) So that all would be equal in God's family.

In Todays Society We look at the outward. God looks at the inward. We value popularity. God values character. We look at intelligence. God looks at the heart. We honor those with money. God honors those with integrity. We talk about what we own. God talks about what we give away. We boast about whom we know. God notices whom we serve. We list our accomplishments. God looks for a contrite heart. We value education. God values wisdom. We love size. God notices quality. We live for fame. God searches for humility. Our view is shallow. God's view is deep. Our view is temporary. God's view is eternal.

Consider the roll call
of God's imperfect heroes:
God does it this way for three reasons:
1) To destroy all human pride,
2) So that no one can boast, and
3) So that all would be equal in God's family.
1. Noah who got drunk.
2. Abraham who lied about his wife.
3. Jacob who was a deceiver.
4. Moses who murdered an Egyptian.
5. Rahab who was a harlot.
6. Samson who had serious problems with lust and anger.
7. David who was an adulterer.
8. Paul who persecuted the church.
9. Peter who denied Christ.
"But God chose the foolish things of the world to shame the wise; God chose the weak things of the world to shame the strong. He chose the lowly things of this world and the despised things—and the things that are not—to nullify the things that are, so that no one may boast before him" (I Corinthians 1:27-29)

Proverbs 31: 25-27

25 She is clothed with strength and dignity,
and she laughs without fear of the future.
26 When she speaks, her words are wise,
and she gives instructions with kindness.
27 She carefully watches everything in her household
and suffers nothing from laziness.

"Life is either a daring adventure or nothing at all." ~Helen Keller "Life's journey is not to arrive at the grave safely in a well-preserved body, but rather to skid in sideways at 60 mph, totally worn out, shouting "...holy ****...what a ride!" -- It's not like any of us is getting out of here alive (physically.) Why not go for it?

Isaiah 41:10

10 So do not fear, for I am with you; do not be dismayed, for I am your God.
I will strengthen you and help you; I will uphold you with my righteous right hand.

One night I dreamed I was walking along the beach with the Lord. Many scenes from my life flashed across the sky. In each scene I noticed footprints in the sand. Sometimes there were two sets of footprints, other times there were one set of footprints.

This bothered me because I noticed that during the low periods of my life, when I was suffering from anguish, sorrow or defeat, I could see only one set of footprints.

So I said to the Lord, “You promised me Lord, that if I followed you, you would walk with me always. But I have noticed that during the most trying periods of my life there have only been one set of footprints in the sand. Why, when I needed you most, you have not been there for me?”

The Lord replied, “The times when you have seen only one set of footprints in the sand, is when I carried you.”

If You Set The Example You Don't Have To Set The Rule...

Whatever your mind can conceive you can achieve...

Today I heard some one say the best revenge is success, this is a lie because when you are focused or driven by revenge you are moving backwards therefor bearing no fruits for success because one cannot move forward while focusing on the past. By thriving on vengeance you are literally killing yourself because when you are angry, upset or depressed your body is living in an acidic state which turns your blood into sludge making you a walking heart attack as well as a host for a wealth of other diseases to thrive.

Living in gratitude and forgiveness causes your body to become and remain alkaline that enhances your immune system to grow stronger. Scientists have proven laughter really is the best medicine as studies show those in therapy to smile, find gratitude and forgiveness for at least ten minutes a day were reduced and some removed from medication healing their various illnesses... something to think about.

www.ingramcontent.com/pod-product-compliance
Lightning Source LLC
Chambersburg PA
CBHW041023040526
R18238500001B/R182385PG44116CBX00001B/1
9780692208052